Get Creative with

Polymer Clay

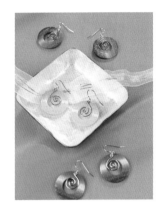

Get Creative with
Polymer Clay

17 step-by-step projects – simple to make, stunning results

EMMA RALPH

NEW HOLLAND

Published in 2006 by
New Holland Publishers (UK) Ltd
London · Cape Town · Sydney · Auckland
www.newhollandpublishers.com

Garfield House, 86–88 Edgware Road, London W2 2EA, United Kingdom

80 McKenzie Street, Cape Town 8001, South Africa

Level 1, Unit 4, 14 Aquatic Drive, Frenchs Forest, NSW 2086, Australia

218 Lake Road, Northcote, Auckland, New Zealand

ISBN 1 84330 986 6

Senior Editors: Clare Sayer, Steffanie Brown
Production: Hazel Kirkman
Design: Glyn Bridgewater
Photographer: Shona Wood
Editorial Direction: Rosemary Wilkinson

10 9 8 7 6 5 4 3 2 1

Reproduction by Pica Digital PTE Ltd, Singapore
Printed and bound by Times Offset (M) Sdn. Bhd., Malaysia

Acknowledgements
The author would like to thank Staedtler (UK) Ltd. for providing the Fimo
polymer clays and Easy Metal used for the projects in this book, as well as
all the other companies that offered their time and support. Special thanks
must also go to Sarah Spivey and Lucy Parter for so kindly modelling for the
"Little princess photo frame" project, and to baby Nicholas O'Hara, whose
portrait graces the "Scrapbooking embellishments" project.

Contents

 Projects

Introduction

Polymer clay is a colourful, easy-to-use modelling material quite unlike any other. It is permanently hardened by baking in a domestic oven and has an abundance of uses, from creating unique beads and jewellery to making mosaics, sculptures, vessels and more. Best of all, no expensive equipment is necessary – your hands, a creative spirit and a few basic tools will be more than enough to start you on your way.

Although I call it "clay" throughout the book, polymer clay is not a clay in the traditional sense. It is made synthetically from pigments, plasticizers and PVC particles that fuse to form a durable plastic when baked. Also, it does not air-dry, so there is never any rush to complete a project. If you wish to take a break, simply cover your work to protect it from dust until you are ready to continue.

After many years of using polymer clay, I have yet to become bored with its seemingly limitless possibilities. There are always new ideas to try out or a new technique to master. I hope this book will inspire you to view polymer clay with the same sense of wonder. The 17 projects in this book will show you, step by step, how to make a variety of gifts, jewellery and items for your home. Do not worry if you have never used polymer clay before – the opening chapters will teach you all the basics and introduce the different materials and equipment used. But do not feel compelled to follow these projects to the letter – if you prefer, adapt the projects and techniques to your own design. After all, there is no right or wrong way to be creative. My hope above all is that you simply have fun with these techniques and projects and that you enjoy creating with polymer clay!

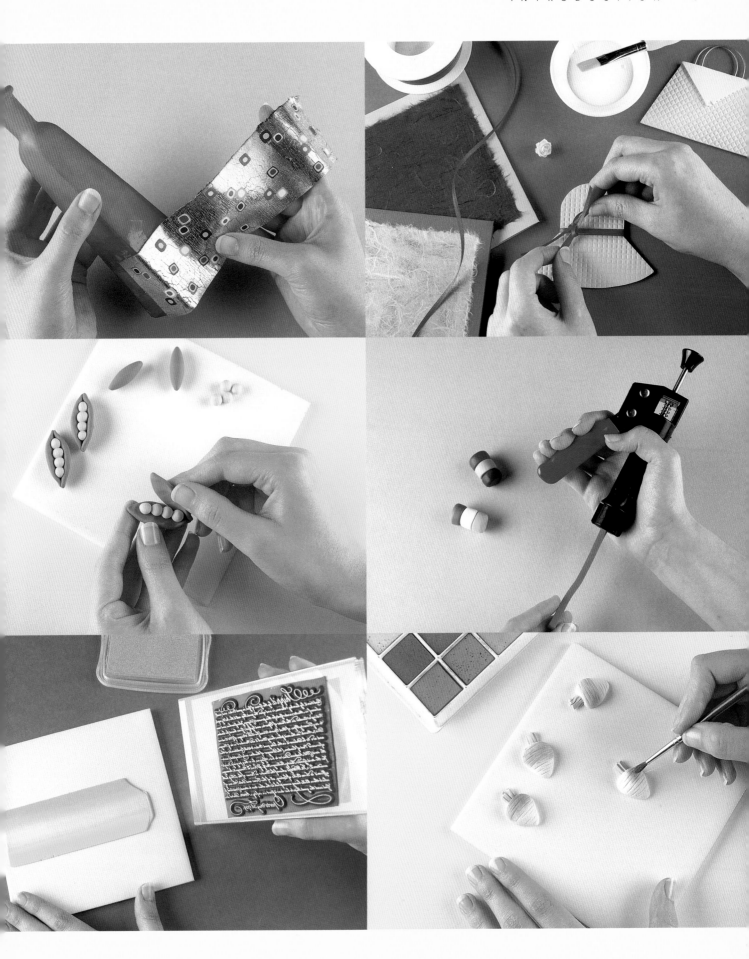

Tools

You will need very few tools to work with polymer clay. Most projects require little more than a smooth work surface and tools to roll, cut and pierce the clay. Although some of the projects require additional tools, you likely have most of these already; the rest can be found in kitchenware or craft stores.

Ceramic tiles Ceramic tiles make ideal work surfaces. You can create a project on a tile, turning it around to work at any angle, and then place it straight into the oven for baking without disturbing the clay.

Baking tray A metal baking tray provides an alternative baking surface. Use baking parchment to line the tray to prevent having a shiny patch where the item being baked touches the tray.

Pasta machine These wonderful machines can roll out even clay sheets in various thicknesses. Different pasta machines have different settings, however, so make and bake test tiles of clay to determine the thickness each setting will produce. While these machines are not essential, they do make life

easier. Check on-line auctions and charity shops – you will be surprised how many pasta machines are up for adoption!

Hand roller For rolling sheets by hand or for smoothing surfaces, use an acrylic roller. Some clay artists use a drinking glass as a roller, but I would urge against this. Glass can break unexpectedly, so why risk injuring your hands when alternatives are readily available? Acrylic rollers cost little and are a wise investment.

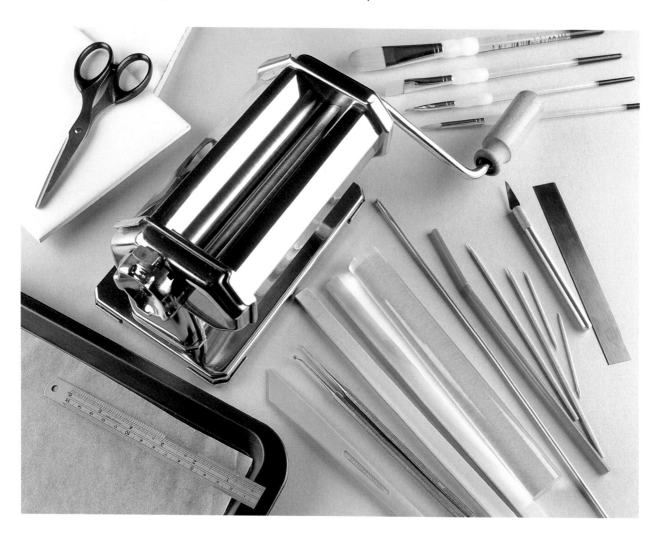

Rolling guides If you don't have a pasta machine, you can make rolling guides from strips of wood or cardboard to help hand-roll clay sheets to an even thickness. For the projects, you will need pairs of guides in the following thicknesses: 1 mm ($\frac{1}{32}$ in), 1.5 mm ($\frac{1}{16}$ in), 2 mm ($\frac{3}{32}$ in) and 4 mm ($\frac{5}{32}$ in).

Tissue blade These sharp, flexible blades are used to cut straight or curved lines in clay sheets, and to slice millefiore canes.

Craft knife A craft knife is needed for cutting more intricate shapes.

Piercing tools Wooden toothpicks, skewers and knitting needles all make excellent piercing tools. Plastic drinking straws can be used to cut larger holes.

Modelling tools A ball stylus, dental pick and other modelling tools can be used to add detail to projects.

Metal ruler Use a metal ruler for measuring, or when cutting long lines in clay with a craft knife. The plasticizers in clay will melt most plastic rulers.

Paintbrushes Choose soft-bristled paintbrushes to apply powders, paints and glue. A stiff-bristled brush is also needed for some effects. There is no need to buy top of the range – economy brushes will do!

Scissors Keep an old pair of scissors handy for cutting out paper templates or for snipping yarns and ribbons.

Extruders An extruder is a highly useful tool for making clay string and logs in various shapes. There are different types of extruders available, all with a barrel, a plunger and a selection of pierced dies. The extruder used in this book was originally designed for sugarcraft. It works on a similar principle to the better-known metal extruders, but has a lever-operated plunger. Using an extruder is not kind on the hands, so be sure to use well-conditioned clay, and only fill the barrel with as much clay as you need. Clean inside the barrel after use with a soft rag to remove any clay residue

Cutters Cookie and craft cutters are superb for cutting interesting shapes from clay sheets and for making simple millefiore canes.

Rubber stamps Rubber stamps make versatile clay tools. Use them simply to texture unbaked clay, or with ink to stamp images over baked or unbaked clay. Some companies sell sheets of unmounted stamps, which offer great value for money. Cut the stamps apart and temporarily stick your chosen stamp to an acrylic block with a glue stick. When you have finished stamping, remove the stamp and wash off the glue.

Push moulds Using push moulds is an easy way to create multi-dimensional clay motifs. Choose flexible moulds where possible, as they are the easiest to use. Several manufacturers offer a range of moulds specifically designed for polymer clay use. There is also a large range of attractive and often highly detailed sugarcraft moulds that work well with polymer clay.

Texture tools Coarse sandpaper and plastic embroidery canvas are just two cheap and cheerful materials that are used to texture the clay in some of the projects. Look out also for lacy fabrics, moulded glass or embossed papers to build up your own unique texture library.

Materials

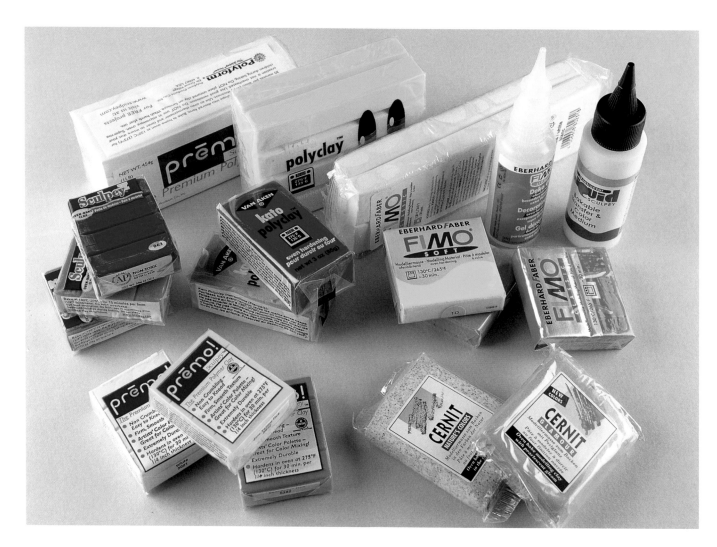

Polymer clay

Several different brands of this remarkable clay are available. Each brand offers a range of inter-mixable colours, and often includes specialities such as stone effect, fluorescent or glow-in-the-dark. Most ranges also contain metallic and pearlescent colours, and usually offer at least one translucent formulation. Most (but not all) brands are sold in small blocks weighing around 60 grams (2 ounces). For the purposes of the projects in this book, a "block" refers to this amount.

Polymer clay quantities

*Based on a small
60 gram / 2 ounce block*

Block	Grams	Ounces
1	60	2
1/2	30	1
1/4	15	1/2
1/8	7.5	1/4
1/16	3.75	1/8
1/32	2	1/16
1/64	1	1/32

However, as most clays are also available in larger blocks, the table on the left gives the approximate weight equivalents for the quantities used should you need them.

Brands of polymer clay

Although several are available, no one brand of polymer clay is "best" overall; essentially, they all contain the same ingredients and have broadly similar properties. That said, some characteristics do vary between brands, such as the clay's softness in use or its strength and flexibility when baked. So, try to use whichever best suits the particular project in hand. Below are some widely available clays and their characteristics – experiment with as many as possible to develop your own feel for each of them.

Fimo Classic (Eberhard Faber): A firm clay that holds detail well, it is strong and flexible after baking but requires more conditioning than most clays and can be difficult to smooth.

Fimo Soft (Eberhard Faber): A soft, easy-to-use clay that smoothes well. Current formulations are brittle after baking, so are not the best choice for projects that require great strength or flexibility.

Premo! Sculpey (Polyform Products Co.): A medium-soft clay that conditions easily. Strong and very flexible when baked, it is a good choice for delicate items and smoothes well.

Sculpey III (Polyform Products Co.): A soft, smoothable and easy-to-condition clay. It is brittle after baking, so it is not recommended for projects where strength or flexibility is required.

Kato Polyclay (Van Aken): A firm but easy-to-condition clay, it holds detail well and is strong after baking. Standard blocks are larger than most brands, offering good value for your money.

Cernit (T & F Kunstoffe): A crumbly clay that conditions quickly, this clay becomes very soft, but is not easily smoothed. It is very strong when baked with a semi-translucent finish.

Scrap clay
This term refers to all the scraps of clay leftover from projects that will not mix together into a nice, re-usable colour. Never throw this scrap clay away! It can be used inside beads, or hidden underneath different surface decorations.

Liquid polymer mediums
Commonly called liquid polymer clay, these mediums have the consistency of honey. They too must be baked, resulting in either a hard or a slightly rubbery finish depending on the brand used. Liquid clay is very useful for joining separate pieces of baked or unbaked clay together, forming a strong bond when baked. Most liquid clays available are translucent formulations. When used in thin layers, they become almost transparent and have myriad decorative uses, from creating image transfers to acting as bakable glazes. They can also be used to embed inclusions such as glitter or small beads, and can be coloured with pigment powders or a little oil paint. Most brands come with a detailed leaflet full of techniques and project ideas, as well as baking instructions that should be followed closely.

Storing polymer clay
Polymer clay will stay useable for years if it is kept cool and stored away from bright light. It does not air-dry, but should nonetheless be kept dust-free, sealed up in polythene bags or wrapped in baking parchment. Do not use normal paper to wrap polymer clay as it leaches out the plasticizers, leaving the clay crumbly and difficult to use. Be careful also with plastic containers – the clay can react when placed with some types of plastic, softening it into a sticky mess!

Embellishments
There are many products you can use to embellish polymer clay. Anything "acrylic" or water-based is likely to be chemically compatible, but there are other products you should avoid. Most solvent-based paints and varnishes do not work with polymer clay – some never dry; others become yellow or tacky over time. Oil paints are also problematic, although they can be used to colour liquid clays and epoxy resins. The embellishments below are all used in the projects, and can be found in most craft stores.

Decorative metal leaf can be applied to unbaked clay for an opulent effect. To apply, lay the leaf over the clay and smooth it down with a soft brush. The clay can then be used as it is, or it can be rolled thinner, for a crackled effect. The leaf also looks beautiful mixed into or layered with translucent clay. Metal leaf should always be varnished after baking for protection.

Mica pigment powders are finely ground, iridescent and metallic powders that add incredible shimmer to projects. They can be brushed over unbaked clay or mixed into liquid clay, varnish or epoxy resin. It is a good idea to varnish powdered clay after baking to protect the colours and to make them more vibrant.

but enamelled and uncoated wires should be removed after baking and glued back into place with superglue.

Glitter can be rubbed over unbaked clay or mixed into translucent clay (both liquid and normal), varnish or epoxy resin. Some brands shrivel or become dull when baked, so place a small pile of glitter on to a ceramic tile and test-bake to check that it will withstand heat before using.

Beads and rhinestones can be attractive embellishments for completing jewellery projects. Those that are made of heat-proof materials, such as metal, stone, pearl, shell, glass or ceramic, can also be embedded and baked into the clay as embellishments.

Epoxy resins (cold enamels) are pourable plastics that solidify with the addition of a liquid hardener. Available clear or ready-coloured, they can create beautiful, glass-like effects on baked polymer clay. The correct ratio of hardener to resin varies between brands, and must be followed exactly. If too little hardener is added, the resin will not set. If too much is used, the resin sets but remains permanently tacky.

Rubber stamping ink can be stamped over baked or unbaked clay. Images stamped with permanent ink will dry very quickly. Pigment ink also works, but it takes much longer to dry. Most pigment inks can be heat-set. So, when they are used on unbaked clay, they will dry as the piece is baked, if not before.

Acrylic paints can also be used on baked or unbaked clay, but do not use them to colour liquid clay or epoxy resins as they are not compatible.

Decorating chalks can be brushed or dabbed directly on to unbaked clay. They are particularly useful for building up colour gradually, adding subtle shading to projects. Some colours can change with the baking process, so it is a good idea to make and bake test tiles using different colours to see how they react to the heat of baking.

Ribbons and yarns make attractive adornments for polymer clay projects. They can be incorporated and baked into projects, or attached after baking with PVA glue.

Craft wire can be embedded into unbaked clay and will survive the baking process. Plastic coated wires often bond with the clay as it bakes,

Coloured cardstock, paper and greetings card blanks are useful for a range of projects, as are larger scrapbooking papers. Colours and styles of paper products vary, so the paper or cardstock you use is very much a personal choice. That said, you should choose products that are made specifically for paper crafts, as they will be of archival quality and are designed to last.

Additional Supplies

These materials may seem rather unexciting, but they are all useful items that you will need for various projects. You will find these products in supermarkets, hardware or craft stores.

PVA glue is a white crafting glue that dries clear and flexible. Use it to bond baked clay with porous materials such as paper, fabric and wood. PVA also helps unbaked clay stick when covering non-porous surfaces such as glass, metal and ceramic, and can also be used to seal wood.

Superglue (cyanoacrylate glue) is used to bond baked clay with nonporous materials. A subtle glue, small drops can be used almost invisibly. It is ideal for gluing metal wires into visible areas of projects. The bond formed is strong but brittle, so do not use if the join will be subjected to heavy handling.

Epoxy glue is also used to attach baked clay to nonporous materials, giving a stronger and more flexible bond than superglue. This type of glue is ideal for attaching pin or barrette backings. Like epoxy resin, it comes in two parts that must be mixed together to activate the glue.

Varnish is used over baked clay to protect surface decoration or to add a glossy finish. Clay manufacturers produce compatible varnishes, but you can also use most acrylic types. Avoid solvent-based and aerosol varnishes, which usually do not dry on polymer clay.

Methylated spirit or rubbing alcohol is used to clean tools, work surfaces and baked or unbaked clay.

Talcum powder or cornstarch both make a good release powder for dusting into push moulds. They can also be dusted over blades to lessen drag when cutting clay.

Graph paper is superb for making simple templates and for marking out grids in clay sheets.

Tracing paper is used for tracing designs to make see-through templates.

Baking parchment can be used to line baking trays and to wrap unbaked clay.

Wet/Dry sandpaper is used to sand baked clay. This waterproof sandpaper is usually black, and is thus distinguishable from other sandpapers. It comes in a variety of grits; the lower the number, the coarser the paper. Papers ranging between 600 and 1200 grit are adequate for most clay-sanding jobs.

Clingfilm can be used to create bevelled edges when cutting clay.

Aluminium foil that is compressed and modelled into solid forms makes excellent armatures for the insides of projects. These forms are particularly useful where weight is a factor, or if you wish to save clay.

Polyester batting, available from haberdasheries, usually in a 1-2 cm ($3/8$-$3/4$ in) thickness, can provide a soft bed upon which to bake delicate objects. Take care that the batting is non-flammable, and be aware that some older types of batting can singe at the baking temperature and even release toxic fumes, so be sure to buy new.

Techniques

The following pages introduce all the basic techniques you will need to approach the projects in this book with confidence. You will be amazed at the variety of effects you can achieve by combining these different techniques.

Conditioning clay

Before starting a project, polymer clay must be kneaded or "conditioned" to make it soft and workable. To do this, either knead the clay between your hands, or run slices cut from the block through a pasta machine until the clay is pliable and folds without cracking.

Rolling logs

Logs are fundamental to many projects, so rolling even logs is a skill well worth mastering. Pinch the clay into a rough log shape and roll it along the work surface to refine and lengthen. Use the entire length of your fingers to roll, and keep your hands moving along the log to prevent bumps forming. Clay string can be made by rolling a small log thinner with your fingertips, or by using an extruder (see page 9).

Rolling and piercing balls

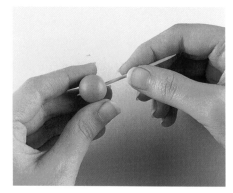

Balls are formed by rolling clay between your palms. This action is almost instinctive, but rolling near-perfect balls does take practice. Clever use of logs can help determine the ball's final diameter. For a 15-mm (5/8-in) ball, form a log 15 mm (5/8 in) in diameter and cut off a section of the same length. Roll this into a ball and it will be pretty close to the required size. To make tiny balls, cut sections from clay string and roll between your fingertips. When making beads, you will want to pierce neat holes into clay balls. Twist a piercing tool into the ball and stop just as the tip starts to emerge on the opposite side. Remove the tool and pierce from this point back towards the middle to complete the hole neatly.

Rolling sheets and strips

The easiest way to roll clay sheets is with a pasta machine. Flatten the clay into a wad and roll it out using the thickest setting on the machine. Re-roll the sheet thinner if required. Sheets can also be hand-rolled with an acrylic roller. To keep the sheet even, roll along guides of the required thickness set on either side of the clay. Where a long strip of clay is needed, fold a sheet in half and re-roll it from the short edge to lengthen it.

Wrapping and cutting seams

For some projects, you will need to wrap clay sheets around an object – for example, when covering a bottle or making millefiore canes. Cut a neat starting edge to the sheet and wrap it right around the object until you meet the starting edge again. Push the overlapping sheet down on to the starting edge to indent a mark on the underside of the clay. Trim along this mark and butt the cut edges together neatly. Where possible, smooth away the seam. If surface decoration prevents the clay being smoothed, a well-matched seam gives the neatest finish.

Making and using templates

Some projects ask you to cut squares or rectangles from clay sheets. You can measure and cut these out with a metal ruler and a craft knife, but it is easier to make a graph paper template to cut around. There are other templates at the back of the book for the more complicated shapes used. Either photocopy or trace the template, then cut it out with a craft knife and a metal ruler. Traced templates are easier to position properly on the clay, as they are see-through. When cutting around templates, use a tissue blade to cut straight lines and a craft knife for the more intricate areas. Try to keep both types of blade as upright as possible for a neater finish.

Colour mixing

Like paints, polymer clays can be mixed together to create any colour imaginable. When mixing, start with the lightest colour first and add in darker colours gradually. Polymer clay colours are usually quite saturated, and it takes very little of the stronger colours to alter the mix. Knead the different colours together (or run them through the pasta machine) until the new colour is uniform, and remember to note the proportions used so you can mix the same colour again. Because the action is the same, you can combine colour mixing and conditioning the clay into a single step when making customised colours.

Colouring translucent clays

Some of the projects in this book require coloured translucent clay. This is easily made by mixing a little coloured clay in with the translucent

clay as you are conditioning it for use. You only need tiny amounts of coloured clay to tinge translucent clay – using too much can lessen the translucent properties of the clay. Coloured translucent clays also tend to darken during the baking process, so when tinting translucent clay, remember that less is more!

Marbling

Colours can also be marbled. To do this, roll two or more colours into logs and twist them together. Roll the clay into a long log and fold it in half, twisting the two halves together. Continue rolling, folding and twisting the clay until it becomes marbled. The marbled log can then be used as it is, or it can be flattened and rolled into a sheet.

Blending clay

A particularly attractive colour-mixing technique is to blend together different colours of polymer clay. This blended clay can be much more interesting in projects than single-colour sheets, as the Glittery bookmarks and Pastel notebook cover projects show (see pages 36 and 48). Blended clay is great for making millefiore canes, too!

Both the Overlap and the Skinner blending techniques explained and demonstrated below can be hand-rolled with an acrylic roller and guides, but it is quicker and easier to use a pasta machine. If you do roll the clay by hand, however, be sure to always roll lengthways away from the fold and never side to side.

The Overlap blend

The Overlap blend allows you to quickly blend numerous colours into hazy, striped sheets. It is particularly suited to making small blends with a broad range of colours.

1 Roll the colours you wish to blend together into small logs, bearing in mind that the thinner the logs are, the closer together the bands of colours will be in the finished blend. Flatten the logs down with your fingertips and lay them together, overlapping their edges slightly.

2 Roll the logs out together lengthways into a sheet. Fold the sheet in half, folding it top to bottom. Then, starting from the fold, roll the clay out lengthways back into a sheet.

3 Repeat the process several more times, always folding and rolling the clay in the same direction until all the colours have blended together.

The Skinner blend

More subtly gradated sheets can be made by creating a Skinner blend (named after artist Judith Skinner, who developed the technique).

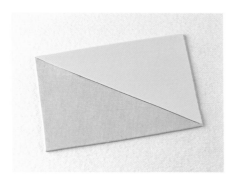

1 Roll two differently coloured clay sheets and form a right-angled triangle from each. This can be done by cutting a triangle freehand from one sheet and using it as a template to cut the second. Or, if you are rolling with a pasta machine and the sheets are quite square, you can

simply cut each sheet in half diagonally and stack the two halves together to make the triangles. When the two triangles are formed, position them together into a rectangle.

2 Carefully fold the rectangle in half top to bottom, then roll it, fold first, back into a sheet. Continue folding and rolling the clay in the same way, always folding in half top to bottom and rolling lengthways from the fold.

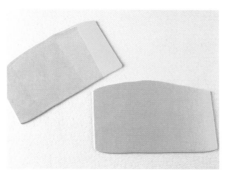

3 After several repetitions, the sheet will start to show bands or stripes of different colours. Continue folding and rolling the sheet a few more times, and the colours will completely blend together. You can then use the blended sheet as it is, or fold it in half once more and roll it from the narrow end to lengthen into a long blended strip. This allows you to spiral the strip up and use it in canes, or concertina the clay to make a blended block of clay.

Mokume gane

Mokume gane (literally "wood grain metal") is a Japanese metalworking technique adapted for use with polymer clay. In this technique, thin layers of different-coloured clays are stacked on top of each other to form a slab. The layers are then distorted so that slices cut horizontally from the top of the slab reveal unique patterns. You can then use these patterned slices and the remaining slab itself decoratively in your clay projects.

Mokume gane slabs are particularly attractive when made from translucent clays interlaced with decorative metal leaf. For the Mokume gane trinket box project on page 72, you will need to make two different translucent mokume gane slabs using the directions below. Keep in mind that these techniques can be adapted by substituting thin layers of normal, opaque polymer clay for the translucent clay and metal leaf to give a different effect.

Translucent mokume gane

1 Cut a block of translucent clay in half. Tint one half of the block with a

pinch of coloured polymer clay of your choice to make your own coloured translucent clay (see page 15). Leave the remaining half of the

the overall pattern. When the slab
has been indented all over, remove
and discard the clingfilm.

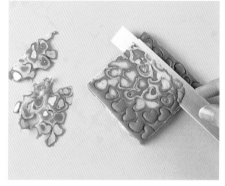

translucent clay block uncoloured,
but condition it as normal to make
the clay soft and pliable.
2 Roll both pieces of clay into square
sheets, each approximately 1 mm
(¹⁄₃₂ in) thick. Cut each sheet into
quarters to make eight small sheets,
and cover all but one with silver
metal leaf. You may find it easier to
apply the metal leaf if you cut it first
to match the size and shape of the
small clay sheets. To do this, cut the
entire booklet of metal leaf sheets to
the correct shape with a pair of
scissors before removing the sheets
from the protective paper and
plastic packaging.
3 With the metal leaf uppermost,
stack the clay sheets on top of each
other, alternating the colours, to form
a slab. Lay the sheet without the
metal leaf coating last, using it as a
cover so the slab both starts and
finishes with a layer of clay, and not
metal. Trim the edges of the slab with

a tissue blade to neaten, and save the
scraps. (Mokume gane scraps are
too good for your normal scrap clay
pile; rolled into balls and pierced,
they make stunning beads.)
4 Lay a piece of clingfilm over the
slab. Push down firmly into the clay
with small craft or cookie cutters to
impress patterns over the slab,
distorting the different layers. The
clingfilm prevents the cutters from
slicing into the clay too cleanly, giving
more distortion and greater variety to

5 Using a sharp tissue blade, cut
slices horizontally from the slab. As
you cut the slices, you will find that
the first few pieces will be the most
dramatic. Set these aside to be used
last on projects, providing a focal
point, and keep cutting more slices.
Arrange the slices over sheets or
balls of clay and roll smooth to create
fantastic metallic effects.

6 Once baked, the effects of translucent mokume gane become most pronounced if you wet-sand the clay smooth and then coat it with some glossy varnish. This will bring out the colours and the depth of the translucent clay.

Making millefiore canes

Millefiore (literally "thousand flowers") is an Italian term describing colourful glassware made using age-old processes adapted by polymer clay artists to make polymer clay Millefiore canes. Millefiore canes are colourful logs of clay that reveal a pattern or picture in the cross section when cut. Slices taken from these canes can be used to decorate projects, or to make attractive beads and charms.

Canes are made by bundling together differently coloured polymer clay logs and sheets. These canes can then be reduced, stretching them longer and thinner to make the pattern smaller. Sections of reduced canes can then also be bundled together to make evermore complex canes. Below are a few simple cane designs to introduce the technique, although you will no doubt wish to experiment with your own designs soon enough. When making your own canes, choose colours with contrasting values (how light or dark the colours are), so that the pattern remains distinct even when the cane is reduced.

Reducing canes

Canes are reduced to a smaller diameter by stretching, rolling, pinching and pulling. Squeeze the

cane evenly, coaxing and pulling the clay out longer and thinner. Round canes can also be rolled gently along the work surface to lengthen them. Square canes should be pinched and pulled out longer, and the edges periodically neatened with a hand roller to keep them in shape. When you reach the desired diameter, trim away the distorted ends to reveal the cane's reduced pattern.

Bull's eye cane

Roll a log and wrap it in contrasting sheets to build up the ringed pattern. To create a more complex, cellular pattern, reduce the cane and cut it into several sections. Bundle these sections together and then reduce, cut and bundle the cane once more.

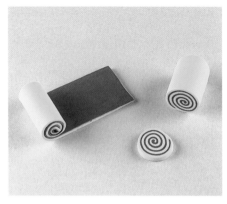

Spiral cane

Lay two contrasting clay strips on top of each other. Flatten one of the narrow edges to a tapered point and, starting from here, roll the clay into a tight spiral.

Cookie-cutter cane

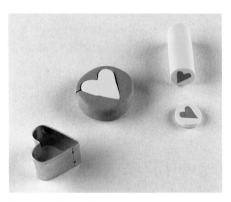

Use small cookie cutters to make pairs of co-ordinating canes. Form two contrasting clay patties, each large enough to accommodate the cutter. Cut the shape from the middle of each and swap the cut out sections. Push the clay back together and reduce the canes.

Striped cane

Lay two contrasting sheets on top of each other. Cut the sheets into equal strips and then stack them together, alternating the colours. To keep the lines crisp, do not reduce striped

canes. Slices cut from striped canes can also be added to other canes to give them a stripy layer.

Geometric cane

Use an extruder to make components for geometric canes. Square and triangular logs can be bundled together to make checkerboard, mosaic or quilt designs quickly and easily.

Extruded cane

Extruding multi-coloured clay plugs creates a bull's eye cane effect in the extruded clay. Form several balls of different colours and push them together into a plug, then load this into the extruder. The colour placed nearest the die will become the outermost colour of the extruded cane, but the colours and pattern inside will vary along its length. Cut and bundle different extruded cane sections together to make wacky composite canes.

Cutting and using cane slices

Slice canes with a sharp tissue blade. Keep the blade as upright as possible as you cut down, and turn the cane regularly to stop it from becoming

flat along the bottom. Thick cane slices can be pierced or fitted with top pins to make beads and charms. Cover balls or sheets of scrap clay with thinner slices and roll smooth to make attractive beads or patterned clay "fabrics".

Baking

Projects are permanently hardened by baking in a domestic oven. It is important that they bake at the correct temperature and for the correct length of time. Under-baked clay will be fragile, while over-baked clay can discolour, burn, and even release dangerous fumes if the recommended temperature is exceeded (see safety advice, right). Most brands bake at around 130° C / 275° F for 30 minutes, although exact requirements vary between brands. Always follow the manufacturer's directions. Use a pre-heated oven unless the specific project states otherwise, and use an independent oven thermometer to verify the baking temperature. The inbuilt thermostats in many ovens can be wildly inaccurate.

Bake projects on a ceramic tile or on a metal baking tray. Keep in mind that the clay will develop a shiny patch wherever it is in contact with the hot baking tray or tile. This does not matter if that part of the project will be hidden anyway, but if it will be on view, this can be prevented by lining the tray or tile with baking parchment. Awkwardly shaped items can be baked supported on a bed of polyester batting, and beads can be suspended on a wire-mesh bead rack. Once baked, the clay must return to room temperature to fully harden, so always allow projects to cool completely before handling.

Sanding and varnishing

Baked clay can be sanded to smooth the surface or to neaten cut edges. Use wet/dry sandpaper and, where possible, wet-sand to keep the dust down. Start with a medium paper, such as 600 grit, and progress through to higher grits for an even smoother finish. When wet-sanding, there is no need to sand under running water, which wastes resources. Instead, fill a small basin with water and dip the sandpaper and clay periodically to keep both wet. Adding a drop of dishwashing detergent to the water will keep the sandpaper clog-free.

Like sanding, varnishing is not essential for most projects, but those decorated with powders or metal leaf should be varnished for protection. After making sure the clay is clean, dry and dust-free, apply the varnish with a soft paintbrush. Allow the varnish to dry, then apply a second coat if desired.

Safety advice

Polymer clay is certified as non-toxic when used in accordance with the manufacturer's instructions. There are, however, some safety points to note when using polymer clay and other craft supplies or tools:

- *Polymer clay can burn and release toxic fumes if baked above the recommended temperature. If you accidentally burn the clay (indicated by a terrible smell!), turn off the oven and remove the clay. Ventilate the room and stay out of it until the fumes have cleared.*

- *Always wash your hands well after working with polymer clay. Baked clay is not considered food-safe, so do not use it to make serving bowls. Unless you can wash every trace of clay residue from kitchen tools, do not use them to prepare food again. This is especially true of pasta machines, which are difficult to clean thoroughly.*

- *Follow manufacturers' instructions and safety advice when using any supplies or tools. Wear protective gloves when using any epoxy products, as they are an irritant, and take extra care when using superglue – it can bond skin in seconds. Always wear a dust mask when using any fine powders. Take care with sharp blades and knives and keep them well out of the reach of children.*

Making jewellery

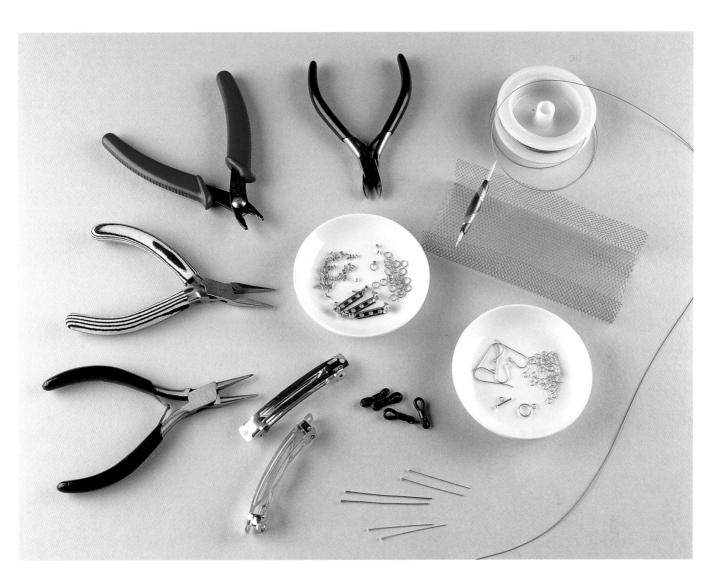

Polymer clay is a versatile medium for making beads and jewellery. If you have never made jewellery before, do not worry! You only need a few tools and findings and some very simple techniques to finish the jewellery projects in this book.

Jeweller's chain-nosed pliers have flat jaws that are used for gripping and bending wire. Because they have no teeth, they will not scratch the wire.

Jeweller's round-nosed pliers have two conical jaws that are used to form loops in wire. The jaws increase in size towards the hinge, allowing you to form loops in a variety of diameters, depending on how far down the jaws you grip the wire.

Wire cutters are used to cut wire. Choose "flush" cutters, as they cut the wire completely blunt, leaving no sharp edges or burs.

Crimping pliers are used to squash crimp tubes neatly when securing necklace and bracelet clasps. They are not essential – you can use chain-nosed pliers instead – but they do give the neatest finish.

Wire-mesh bead racks are easily made from wire mesh. These racks are used to support clay beads that have been threaded on to wooden toothpicks while baking or varnishing. To make a rack, select a mesh with wide holes, then cut out a rectangle and bend the sides up to form walls.

Tigertail is a nylon-coated wire cable used for stringing beads. It is available in different diameters and flexibilities. The more expensive, knot-able versions kink less and give the best finish.

Headpins are wires with a flat pinhead at the end. Thread beads on to these when making dangling earrings, charms or pendants. Finish the piece by turning a simple hanging loop in the end of the wire, or by making a more secure wrapped loop (see right).

Top pins are short lengths of metal wire with a pre-formed loop at one end. Embed and bake them into polymer clay projects to add a hanging loop. Because metal does not bond with clay, they should be removed after baking and glued back into place with a drop of superglue to secure.

Jump rings are circles of wire that are used to link different components together. They can also be added to a pendant or an earring to change the orientation of how the piece hangs.

Earring findings are available in different styles and metals, and for both pierced and un-pierced ears. When buying earring findings, remember that many people are allergic to the metals used in cheaper findings. Real gold and hypo-allergenic metals such as titanium or niobium can be worn by nearly

everyone. Most (but not all) people have no trouble with sterling silver or surgical steel.

Crimps are small, squashable metal tubes or beads used to secure clasps on tigertail. Crimp tubes will give a nicer finish than the cheaper crimp beads, especially if finished with crimping pliers.

Clasps of all types are available to finish necklaces and bracelets. They all have two parts that attach to either end of the necklace or bracelet and join them together. Think about ease of use when choosing clasps. For example, toggle (circle and bar) clasps can be good for bracelets, as they are easy to do up single-handed.

Barrette and pin findings are needed to make polymer clay brooches and hair barrettes. For barrettes, bake the clay in place on the finding to give the clay the correct curve. Remove the clay when cool and glue it back into place with epoxy glue.

Jewellery techniques

Using jump rings
Use two pairs of pliers to grip the metal on either side of the jump ring's opening and twist the ring

open or closed. Do not pull it apart, as this will distort its shape and weaken the metal.

Making a wrapped loop
Finishing a headpin with a wrapped loop is more secure than turning a simple loop, as a wrapped loop cannot be pulled open. To make a wrapped loop, you will need at least 2 cm ($^3/_4$ in) of headpin wire left over after threading on the beads.

1 Leave a 2-mm ($^3/_{32}$-in) gap after the last bead and bend the remaining wire down at a right angle. Hold the headpin at the bend with round-nosed pliers and, using your fingers, push the end of the wire right around the jaw of the pliers to form a loop. When the loop is complete, the tail end of the wire should be sticking out at a right angle to the headpin, ready to wrap around it.

2 Hold the loop flat between the jaws of some chain-nosed pliers. Wrap the tail end of the wire right around the headpin, starting just below the loop. Continue wrapping the wire around and down the headpin to fill up the gap left in step 1.

3 When the wrapping is complete, trim away any leftover wire with a pair of wire cutters. Check that the trimmed end is neat. If it is sharp or sticking out, either squeeze it into place with some chain-nosed pliers or file it down with some sandpaper or a small file.

Attaching clasps using crimp tubes

When making necklaces or bracelets, allow at least 8 cm (3 1/8 in) extra tigertail at each end so you can attach the clasp. You may want to secure one end of the tigertail first, and then thread on all the beads (this is a good method if you know the order in which you wish to thread the beads). Alternatively, you can thread all the beads first and then later attach the clasp to each end. This method allows you to alter the design as you go, and also to work from both ends of the tigertail at once. Take care not to lose the beads off the bottom when threading

though! Whichever method you use, the principles are the same for attaching the clasp to the end of the tigertail.

1 Thread a crimp tube on to the tigertail, then thread on one half of the clasp. Thread the end of the tigertail back through the crimp, trapping the clasp on a small loop of tigertail. The crimp tube will now have two strands of tigertail running through it. Pull the tigertail end taut, and if the beads are already threaded, check along the necklace to make sure there are no gaps.

2 Squash the crimp with crimping pliers or chain-nosed pliers to lock the tigertail in place. Squashing the crimp with crimping pliers is a two-part process. First, use the notch nearest the plier's hinge to squash

the crimp tube into a figure-of-eight shape, trapping one strand of tigertail in each loop on the figure eight. Finish the crimp by squashing it in the pliers' second notch, folding the loops of the figure eight over on themselves neatly. With the clasp secure, thread the remaining tigertail back through the beads to hide.

Hat and handbag greetings cards

Polymer clay is a wonderful medium for making decorations to adorn greetings cards. Use the hat and handbag templates to create these two attractive cards, or adapt the project and make cards of your own design. Any simple shape that can be cut out and embellished will work well for this project.

"Not only are they fun to make, these cards are fun to give too, and they are much more personal than shop-bought cards."

You will need

Materials

- ½ block of pale yellow polymer clay
- ½ block of pink polymer clay
- 16 cm (6¼ in) of pink craft wire, 1.5-mm diameter (14 gauge)
- Fuchsia ribbon rose, 15 mm (⅝ in)
- One piece each of 15 x 21-cm (6 x 8-in) pink and navy mulberry papers
- PVA glue
- Blank red greetings card, 144 x 144 mm (5⅝ x 5⅝ in)
- Blank blue greetings card 144 x 144 mm (5⅝ x 5⅝ in)
- Pale blue ribbon rose, 15 mm (⅝ in)
- 30-cm (12-in) length of red ribbon, 3 mm (⅛ in) wide

Tools

- Pasta machine (optional)
- Hand roller
- Metal ruler
- 2 ceramic tiles
- section of plastic embroidery canvas, 12 x 12 cm (4¾ x 4¾ in)
- Hat and handbag (body and flap) templates (see page 92), traced and cut out
- Craft knife
- Wire cutters
- Tissue blade
- Medium-sized glue stick or similar-shaped object (to act as a former)

1 Roll the yellow clay into a sheet 2 mm (³/₃₂ in) thick. Taking care not to trap any air bubbles beneath the clay, lay the sheet on a tile. Place a piece of plastic embroidery canvas over the clay surface and roll over it with a hand roller to texture the clay. Remove the canvas.

2 Lay the hat template over the yellow clay sheet and cut around it with a craft knife. Hold the craft knife as upright as you can while cutting for the neatest possible finish. Leave the clay hat in place on the tile, ready for baking, and remove the surplus clay, setting it aside to use later.

3 Roll a pink clay sheet 2 mm ($^3/_{32}$ in) thick and lay it on the second tile. Texture the clay with the embroidery canvas as before, laying the canvas diagonally this time to vary the pattern. Place the handbag template on the clay and cut around it with a tissue blade. Leave the handbag in place on the tile and remove the surplus clay.

4 Cut two 8-cm ($3^1/_8$-in) lengths of craft wire using the wire cutters. Curve the wires around a glue stick or a similarly sized and shaped object to make handles for the handbag. Push the handles into the clay at the top of the handbag, off-setting them slightly so that both are clearly visible. Make sure the handle ends are flush with the clay's surface.

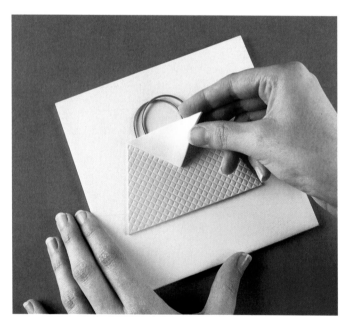

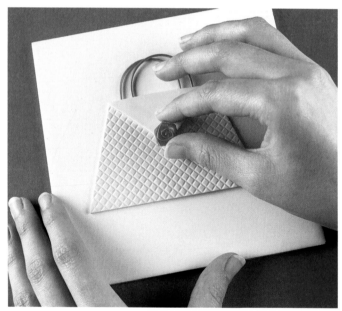

5 Roll a sheet of clay 1.5 mm ($^1/_{16}$ in) thick from the remaining yellow clay. Lay the handbag flap template over the sheet and cut around it with a tissue blade. Carefully lift the handbag flap by sliding a tissue blade underneath the clay and place it on top of the handbag, conveniently hiding the handle's ends.

6 Push the fuchsia ribbon rose into the clay at the base of the handbag flap, making a dent to house the rose after baking. Remove the ribbon rose and bake the hat and handbag in place on their tiles, following the clay manufacturer's recommendations. Allow the baked pieces to cool completely.

7 Tear a square from both the pink and the navy sheets of mulberry paper, each a little smaller than the greetings card's blanks. Tear the paper against a metal ruler to keep the lines straight. Glue the navy paper on to the blue greetings card and the pink paper on to the red card using a thin smear of PVA glue.

8 Wrap the red ribbon twice around the hat and form a small bow. Fix the blue ribbon rose on to the centre of the bow with PVA glue. Glue the fuchsia ribbon rose into the dent in the handbag flap. When both ribbon roses are secure and the glue has dried, glue the hat and handbag motifs to the cards.

Variation

Glittery snowflake cards

If designing templates isn't your thing, try using cookie cutters instead. These cards were made from clay cut out with pretty snowflake cutters and dusted with glitter and mica pigment powders.

Classical barrette

The work of the English potter Josiah Wedgwood inspired this stylish hair barrette. Wedgwood himself borrowed from ancient Greek and Roman art to create his world-famous Jasperware pottery. In this project, we use a push mould to re-create those classical relief effects he made so famous.

"Choose a spray or border design mould for this project, or select several smaller motifs that can be laid out together."

You will need

Materials

- ½ block of pale turquoise polymer clay
- ¼ block of white polymer clay
- Graph paper (optional)
- Talcum powder
- 8-cm (3⅛-in) barrette backing
- Coarse sandpaper
- Epoxy glue

Tools

- Pasta machine or hand roller
- Ceramic tile
- Wooden toothpick
- Metal ruler
- Push mould, with design to fit the barrette surface
- Dull tissue blade
- Extruder
- Soft paintbrush
- Baking tray (optional)
- Protective gloves

1 Roll a turquoise clay sheet 2 mm (³⁄₃₂ in) thick and lay it on a ceramic tile. Cut a rectangle 8 cm (3⅛ in) by 2.5 cm (1 in) using a metal ruler and a craft knife, or by making a graph paper template to cut around with a tissue blade. Leave the rectangle on the tile and remove the surplus clay.

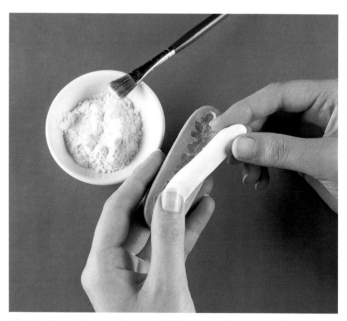

2 Dust the push mould thoroughly with talcum powder and brush out any excess. Estimate the amount of white clay needed to fill the mould and knead it until soft and pliable. Form the clay into a shape roughly similar to the motif (in this case, a short log) and push it firmly into the mould.

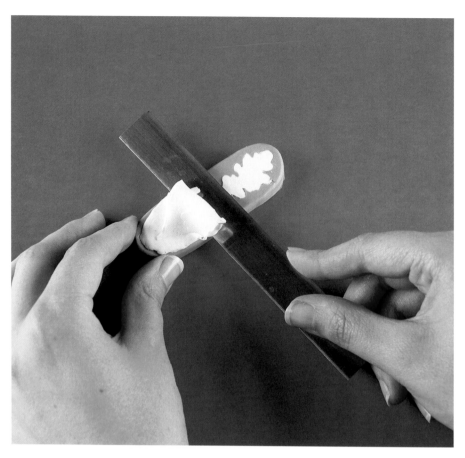

3 When the mould is full, carefully remove the excess clay with an old tissue blade. Flex the blade so it is flush with the back of the mould, and use a gentle sawing motion to slice away the surplus clay. If the blade drags or sticks, dust it with a little bit of talcum powder.

Helpful hint
When removing the excess clay from a mould, always use an old tissue blade, as a brand-new one will be very sharp and can easily cut into the mould without your noticing. Be sure to keep your fingers well away from the blade.

4 Flex the mould slightly to loosen the clay from the sides, then tap the moulded motif out. If the mould is hollow-backed, take care not to push up from underneath with your fingers, as this can distort the motif. If the clay sticks to the mould or distorts, re-mould it using a little more talcum powder, then remove it as before.

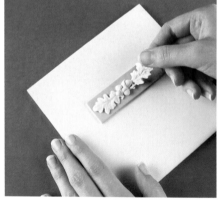

5 Lay the motif on the clay base, as centred as possible. It may help to measure the base and find the exact centre with which to align the middle of the motif. If you have several motifs, lay them out in whichever arrangement you prefer. When happy with the layout, push the moulded clay down gently to adhere it to the base.

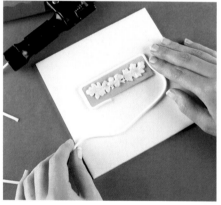

6 Fill the extruder with the remaining white clay. Using a 3-mm (1/8-in) round-holed die, extrude enough string to circle the barrette. Push the string firmly against the clay edge, working right around the barrette. Trim the string where it overlaps and butt the cut edges together neatly, smoothing away the seam with your fingertips.

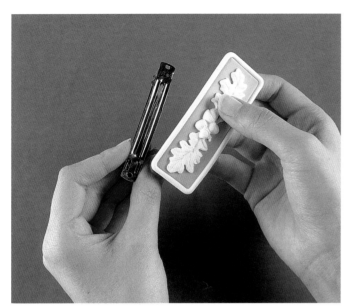

7 Free the barrette from the tile and position it on to the barrette backing. With the barrette in place on the backing, place it onto a ceramic tile or baking tray and bake following the clay manufacturer's instructions. Allow the barrette to cool on the backing, so the clay maintains the correct curve.

8 Use some coarse sandpaper to roughen the surface of the metal barrette backing, providing a "key" to which the glue can adhere. Wearing protective gloves, mix up some epoxy glue, following the manufacturer's directions. Glue the barrette to the backing and allow the glue to set until hard.

Variation

Oriental vessel

This beautiful oriental vessel was made by covering a glass coffee jar with teal polymer clay and adorning it with a variety of moulded motifs.

Butterfly wind chimes

These delightful wind chimes will brighten any room. Hung from window or door frames, the chimes sound gently in the breeze to create a relaxing atmosphere. These wind chimes are shaped using a butterfly cookie cutter, a popular design that can be found in most kitchenware stores, but other shapes can be used as well.

"Wash the cutter well in warm soapy water after use if you want to use it to make cookies again."

You will need

Materials

- ½ block of turquoise polymer clay
- ¼ block of yellow polymer clay
- Set of small turquoise wind chimes
- Metallic turquoise embroidery yarn, 1 m (1 yd)
- Metal loop hanger
- 8 cm (3⅛ in) of turquoise craft wire, 1 mm in diameter (18 gauge)
- Mica pigment powder in interference blue colour
- Superglue
- Varnish

Tools

- Pasta machine or hand roller
- Large ceramic tile
- Butterfly cutter, 8 cm (3⅛ in) in diameter
- Wire cutters
- Jeweller's round-nosed pliers
- Non-flammable polyester batting
- Masking tape (if using enamelled wire)
- Flat-edged modelling tool
- Coarse sandpaper
- Round and tear-drop cutters, each 8 mm (5/16 in) in diameter
- Small and large soft-bristled paintbrushes

1 Roll a turquoise clay sheet 2 mm (3/32 in) thick and lay it on a large ceramic tile. Cut out a butterfly to make the wind chime base and leave it in place on the tile. Remove the surplus clay and roll it into another sheet 2 mm (3/32 in) thick. Press coarse sandpaper over the sheet to texture the clay and cut a second butterfly to make the top of the wind chime.

2 Thread the chimes on to lengths of embroidery yarn. Allowing them to swing freely, secure each chime by knotting the yarn, then trim away the loose ends. Thread the metal hanger on to a length of yarn and knot the two ends together tightly. Continue knotting the threads together several more times to form a simple cord approximately 1 cm (3/8 in) long.

★☆☆ **Skill level** 🕐 **1 hour** **Techniques:** *Cutters p.9, Texture tools p.9, Rolling logs p.14*

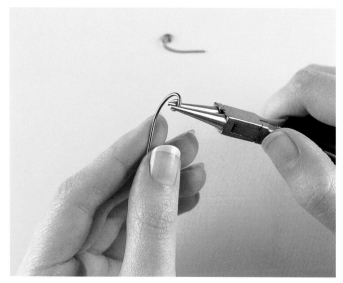

3 Cut two 4-cm (1½-in) lengths of craft wire. Using round-nosed pliers, turn a small spiral in the end of each wire to make the butterfly's antennae. Hold the antennae together to check that they form a matching pair, making adjustments as necessary. If using enamelled wire, wrap the points of the pliers with masking tape to prevent them from marking the wire's coating.

4 Arrange the chimes along the bottom edge of the base butterfly. Push the knots firmly into the clay and support the chimes on some polyester batting. Push the hanger cord into the clay at the top of the base, allowing a little room so the finished wind chime can swing freely. Finally, place the antennae on either side of the hanger, pushing the ends of the wire down into the clay.

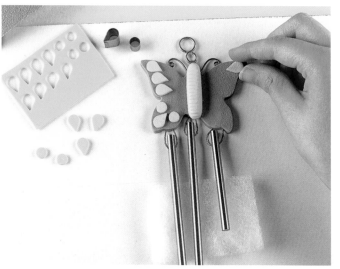

5 Check that all the knots and wires are sunk into the clay and that the base is level. Use a hand roller to gently even out the surface if necessary, but take care not to distort the shape. Carefully place the textured butterfly top over the base butterfly. Push down lightly to adhere it to the clay base below, sandwiching the knots and wires securely between the two clay layers.

6 Roll a yellow log 1 cm (³⁄₈ in) in diameter and long enough to make the butterfly's body. Flatten it slightly and indent horizontal lines with a flat-edged modelling tool. Push the body into place down the centre of the butterfly. Roll a yellow sheet 2 mm (³⁄₃₂ in) thick, and texture with sandpaper. Using the cutters, cut eight tear-drops and four circles and use them to decorate the butterfly's wings as shown.

7 Brush the butterfly all over with the mica pigment powder, then brush away the excess with a large soft paintbrush. The interference colours are translucent and will add an iridescent sheen without drowning out the clay colour beneath.

8 Make sure the chimes are not touching the clay and then bake the butterfly on the tile, following the clay manufacturer's recommendations. When cool, remove the antennae and glue them securely back into place with superglue. Finally, varnish the butterfly to protect and to enhance the powder decoration, and allow the varnish to dry completely.

Variation

Holiday wind chimes

Festive Christmas tree or romantic Valentine's Day wind chimes are just two possible variations to this project. With so many different cutters available, you can make chimes for any and every occasion.

Glittery bookmarks

Delight the bookworms in your life with one of these gorgeous, glittery bookmarks. Not only do they make great gifts, they are also very easy to make – the sparkling motifs are nothing more than holes filled with glitter and translucent liquid clay. Be sure to use a heat-resistant glitter for this project, and choose a strong, flexible clay, so your bookmarks will be durable as well as pretty.

"This technique can also be used to create stained glass effects by simply tinting the liquid clay with oil paints instead of mixing in glitter."

You will need

Materials
- ½ block of coral pink polymer clay
- ½ block of yellow polymer clay
- Translucent liquid clay
- Green glitter
- 60-cm (24-in) length of green ribbon, 3 mm (⅛ in) wide

Tools
- Pasta machine or hand roller
- Metal ruler
- Tissue blade or

- craft knife
- Ceramic tile
- Non-flammable polyester batting
- Drinking straw
- Assortment of small cutters
- Wooden toothpick
- Dental pick (optional)
- Bamboo skewer
- Ceramic mixing dish
- Scissors

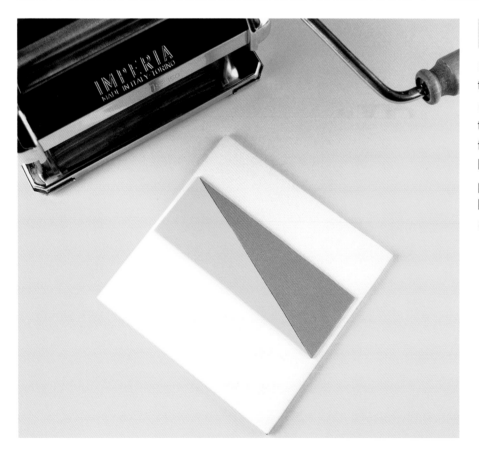

1 Roll the coral pink and yellow clays into sheets 2 mm (³/₃₂ in) thick and cut a right-angled triangle from each that is 14 cm (5½ in) by 5 cm (2 in). Position the triangles into a rectangle and form the rectangle into a Skinner blend, following the directions on page 16. Roll the blended sheet a little thinner, until it is 1.5 mm (¹/₁₆ in) thick.

★☆☆ **Skill level**   🕐 **30 minutes to 1 hour**   **Techniques:** *Rolling and piercing balls p.14, The Skinner blend p.16*

2 Lay the blend on to a ceramic tile, taking care not to trap any air bubbles. Cut out a rectangle 13 cm (5⅛ in) by 4 cm (1½ in) and remove the surplus clay. Use a drinking straw to cut a ribbon hole at the top of the bookmark, cutting at least 5 mm (³⁄₁₆ in) from the edge so there is a strong clay border all around the hole.

3 Use a selection of small cutters to cut shapes into the bookmark, leaving a border of at least 5 mm (³⁄₁₆ in) around each shape for strength. Without disturbing the bookmark, carefully fish out the excess clay with a wooden toothpick or a dental pick to leave neatly shaped holes that are now ready to be filled with glitter.

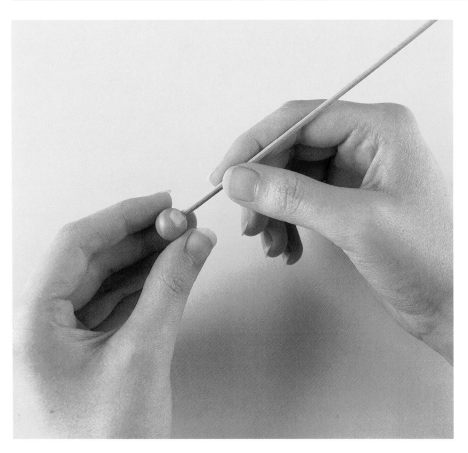

4 Marble together the excess clay removed from the holes. Pinch off some clay and roll a small ball, approximately 10 mm (³⁄₈ in) in diameter. Using a bamboo skewer, pierce the ball to make a bead embellishment for the ribbon. Make sure the hole is large enough to take the doubled-over ribbon. Set the bead aside on some polyester batting, ready for baking.

5 Pour some translucent liquid clay into a ceramic dish and mix in some glitter. Use a wooden toothpick to drop the glittery paste into all the holes except the ribbon hole. Use the toothpick to push the paste close up to the sides of the holes, then allow the paste to settle for ten minutes until it has levelled out and any air bubbles have dispersed.

6 Following the clay manufacturer's directions, bake the pieces in place on their tile and batting, allowing them to cool completely before handling. Fold the ribbon in half to make a loop and thread it through the ribbon hole. Bring the ribbon ends through the loop and knot on the bead to secure. Trim the ribbon ends to a suitable length.

Dragonfly gift tags

These attractive gift tags are very versatile. When used to label gifts, they are sure to be treasured as much as the gift itself, but you can also use them as embellishments for greetings cards or for other paper crafts.

"Try these tags in other colour combinations, too. With so many different inks, powders and coloured wires available, the possibilities are truly limitless."

You will need

Materials

- ⅛ block of turquoise polymer clay
- 28 cm (11 in) of pink craft wire, 1 mm in diameter (18 gauge)
- Mica pigment powder, duo blue/green colour
- Superglue
- Varnish
- Green cardstock, 10 x 15 cm (4 x 6 in)
- Green and blue pigment ink pads
- PVA glue
- 60 cm (24 in) of pink ribbon, 3 mm (⅛ in) wide

Tools

- Metal ruler
- Craft knife
- Tissue blade (optional)
- Ceramic tile
- Wire cutters
- Jeweller's round-nosed pliers
- Paintbrush
- Gift tag template (see page 92), photocopied and cut out
- Pencil
- Dental pick or needle
- Cutting mat
- Hole punch
- Leaf-design rubber stamp, 6 cm (2⅜ in) in diameter
- Flower-design rubber stamp, 15 mm (⅝ in) in diameter
- Wet/dry sandpaper

1 Roll the turquoise clay into a log 10 mm (⅜ in) in diameter. Measuring against a metal ruler, cut two 15-mm (⅝-in) long sections and four 5-mm (³⁄₁₆-in) sections from the log. Cut two of the 5-mm (³⁄₁₆-in) sections in half and then roll each of the sections into smooth, round balls to make two large, two medium and four small balls in total.

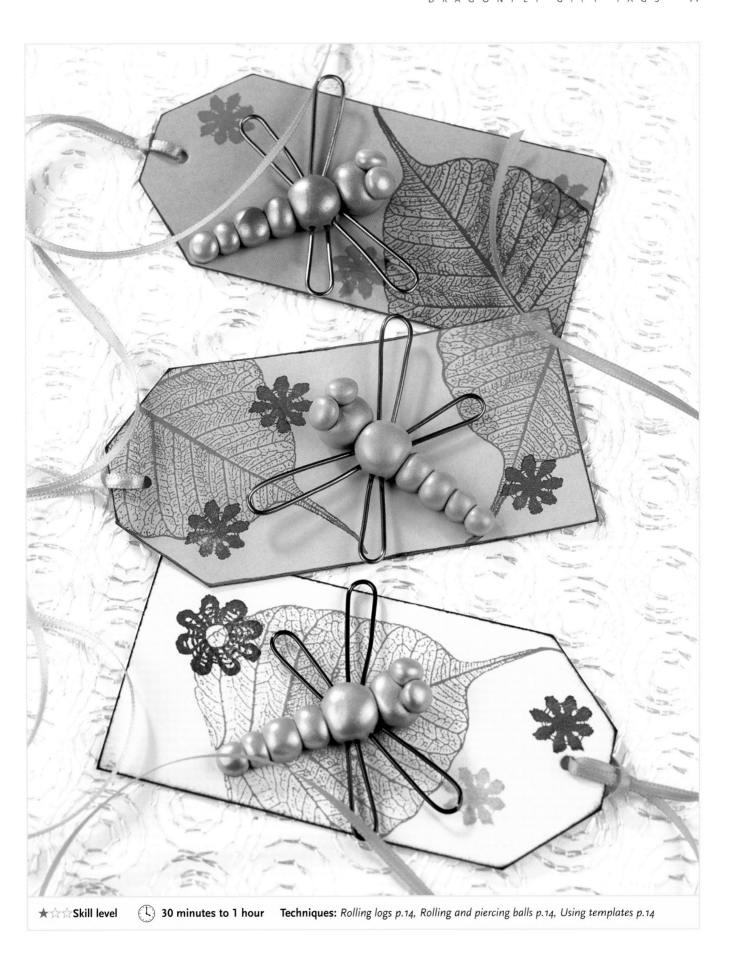

★☆☆**Skill level** 🕐 **30 minutes to 1 hour** **Techniques:** *Rolling logs p.14, Rolling and piercing balls p.14, Using templates p.14*

2 Set two of the smallest balls aside. Working on a ceramic tile, arrange the six remaining balls in a line, from largest to smallest, to form the dragonfly's head and body. Push the balls together so they adhere to each other and then flatten them slightly with your fingertip. Place the two balls kept aside earlier on to the dragonfly's head and push them into place to make the eyes.

3 Use wire cutters to cut two 8-cm (3⅛-in) and two 6-cm (2⅜-in) lengths of craft wire to make the wings. Bend each wire in half around the jaws of the round-nosed pliers to give the wing tips a gentle curve. Push the wings into the dragonfly's body. Place the large wings closest to the head, angled slightly forwards as shown, and the smaller wings just behind, angled backwards.

4 Dust the dragonfly all over with mica pigment powder, and then bake it in place on the tile, following the clay manufacturer's recommendations. When cool, remove the wings and secure them back into place with superglue. Finally, varnish the dragonfly to protect and to enhance the mica pigment powder. Allow the varnish to dry completely.

5 Lay the gift-tag template over the green-coloured cardstock and draw around it with a pencil. Prick through the template with a dental pick or a needle to mark the position of the ribbon hole. Working on a cutting mat, cut out the gift-tag using a craft knife and metal ruler. Use a hole-punch to cut the ribbon hole.

6 Ink the leaf stamp with the green ink pad. Working over scrap paper, stamp over the edge of the cardstock to create partial leaf images at the top and the bottom of the tag. Ink the flower stamp with the blue ink pad and add a few flower images. Rub the green ink pad along each side of the tag, colouring the edge of the cardstock slightly to give the tag definition.

7 Rub the baked dragonfly over the sandpaper to remove any stray powder or varnish from its underside, and to provide a good "key" to which the glue can adhere. Decide where to place the dragonfly and, when happy with the positioning, glue it on to the tag with PVA glue. When the glue has dried completely, attach the pink ribbon to finish.

Calligraphy earrings

These vibrant, blended earrings are sure to get you noticed! Fun to make, they also provide the perfect introduction to rubber stamping on polymer clay. The earrings are patterned using a script-effect rubber stamp and then embellished with simple wirework.

"Any script or print-effect rubber stamp will work for this project; you will find most rubber-stamping stores carry a good selection."

You will need

Materials

- ⅛ block of white polymer clay
- ⅛ block of bright green polymer clay
- ⅛ block of yellow polymer clay
- Silver pigment inkpad
- Script-effect rubber stamp
- 14 cm (5½ in) of silver wire, 1-mm diameter (18-gauge)
- 2 silver jump rings, 6 mm (¼ in) in diameter
- Silver earring findings

Tools

- Pasta machine or hand roller
- Paintbrush
- Ceramic tile
- Round craft cutter, 3 cm (1¼ in) in diameter
- Round craft cutter 1.5 cm (⅝ in) in diameter
- Wooden toothpick
- Wire cutters
- Small jeweller's round-nosed pliers

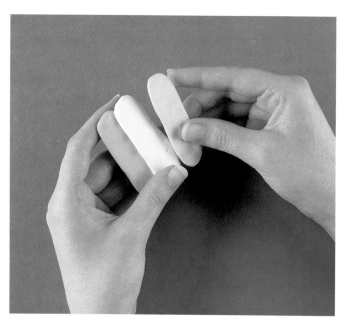

1 Form the white, green and yellow clays into short logs 12 mm (½ in) in diameter and flatten each one down a little with your fingertips. Placing the white clay in the middle, lay the flattened logs together and overlap them slightly, ready to roll out into a simple overlap blend.

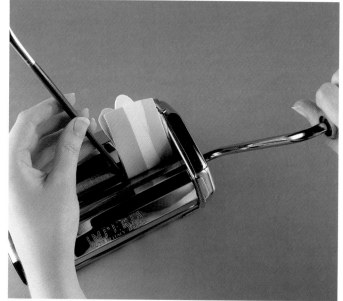

2 Roll the clay out lengthways until it is 2 mm (³/₃₂ in) thick. Fold it top to bottom and roll out again, repeating this until the colours blend. Try to prevent the blend widening too much; use a paintbrush handle to hold the clay close to the side of the pasta machine as you roll.

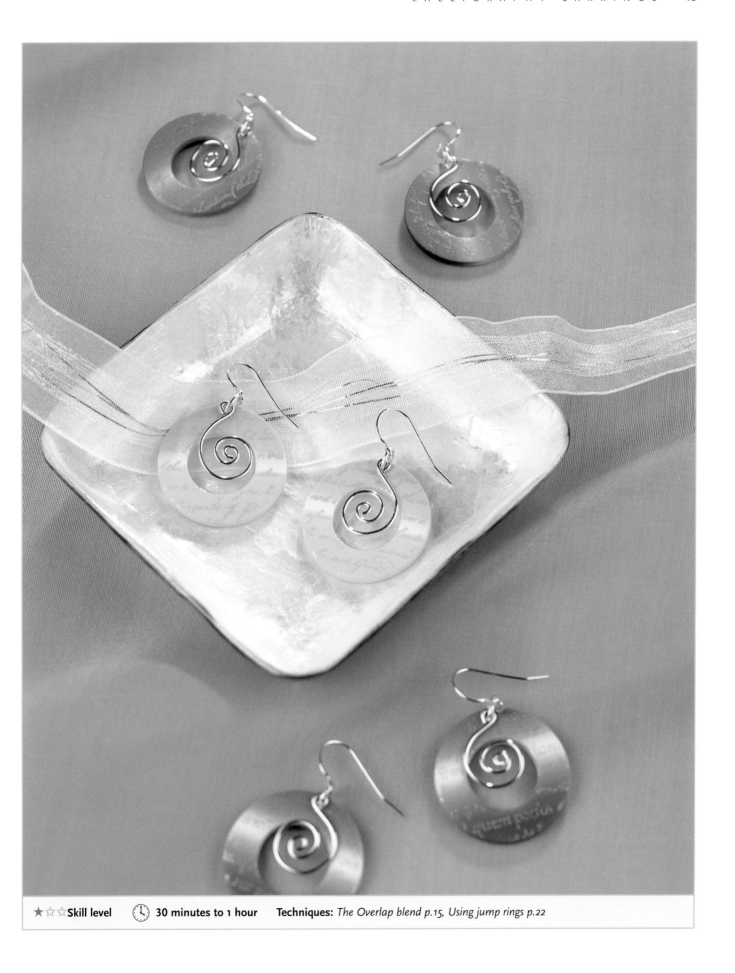

★☆☆ **Skill level**   🕐 **30 minutes to 1 hour**   **Techniques:** *The Overlap blend p.15, Using jump rings p.22*

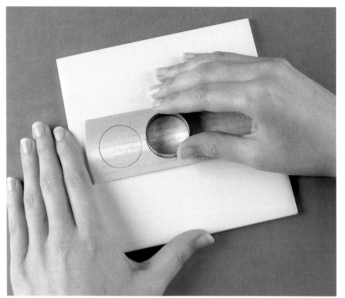

3 Lay the blend on to a ceramic tile. Ink the rubber stamp and stamp over the clay. A light touch will just print the text onto the surface, while pushing more firmly will also indent the pattern, giving a textured effect. The ink can take a while to dry, but if you have a steady hand there is no need to wait, as the ink will heat-set when the clay is baked.

4 Cut two circles with the larger cutter, ensuring that both are cut in line so the colours match in the finished pair of earrings. (There should be enough clay left at this point to cut a third circle should you wish to make a matching pendant.) Leave the earrings in place on the tile and remove the surrounding surplus clay.

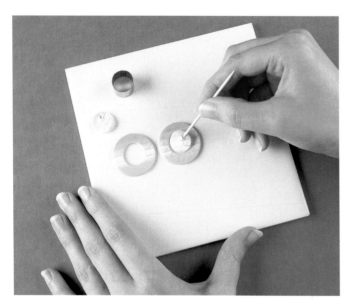

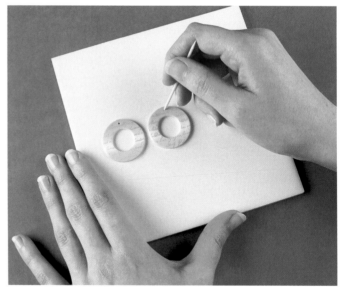

5 Cut a hole in the centre of each earring using the smaller cutter. Rest the cutter on the clay and carefully reposition until you are happy it is centred before pushing down to cut. Leave the earrings in place on the tile and remove the waste clay with a wooden toothpick, taking care to not disturb the earrings as you do so.

6 Make a small hanging hole at the top of each earring with a wooden toothpick. Make sure the hole is at least 2 mm ($3/32$ in) away from the edge; any closer and the clay around the hole will be rendered fragile. Bake the earrings in place on the tile, following the clay manufacturer's recommendations, and allowing them to cool completely before handling.

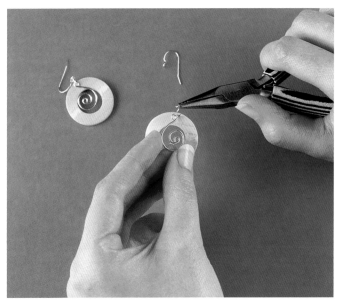

7 Using wire cutters, cut 7 cm ($2^3/_4$ in) of silver wire. Form a loop at one end using a pair of round-nosed pliers. Holding the loop in the pliers, wrap the wire around to form an open spiral. Repeat to make a second, matching spiral and then turn a loop in the tail end of each, working back in the opposite direction, to form hanging loops.

8 Use two pairs of pliers to open the jump rings and attach them to the earrings. Add a wire spiral to the front of each earring and twist the jump rings closed again. Finally, attach the earring findings. To make the earrings face frontward, give the loop on the earring wire a quarter-turn, or alternatively, add another jump ring to the ensemble.

Variation

Matching pendant

An additional clay ring, embellished in the same way as the earrings and hung from a silver necklace wire, makes a stylish matching pendant.

Pastel notebook cover

These stylish polymer clay covers can be made to fit any spiral-bound notebook. Decorated with a small glass mirror and covered in shimmering mica pigment powder, these spectacular covers really will light up the room! The clay amounts given here are enough to cover a notebook of 10 x 15 cm (4 x 6 in). Adjust the amounts accordingly for larger or smaller notebooks.

"Choose a notebook with coloured pages, as the paper will show through the pierced decorations on the clay cover."

You will need

Materials

- 10 x 15-cm (4 x 6-in) cardboard-covered, spiral-bound notebook
- ½ block of white polymer clay
- ¾ block of yellow polymer clay
- Round decorative glass mirror, 2 cm (¾ in) in diameter
- Mica pigment powder in interference gold colour
- Varnish

Tools

- Bulldog clip
- Jeweller's chain-nosed pliers
- Pencil

- Metal ruler
- Dental pick or needle
- Pasta machine (optional)
- Large ceramic tile
- Coarse sandpaper
- Wooden barbecue skewer
- Hand roller
- Tissue blade
- 2 round cutters, one 15 mm (⅝ in) in diameter and the other, 25 mm (1 in) in diameter
- Small ball stylus tool
- Tear-drop cutter, 8 mm (⁵⁄₁₆ in) in diameter
- Extruder (optional)
- Small and large soft-bristled paintbrushes

1 Clip the notebook's pages and back cover together with a bulldog clip. Straighten out the ends of the spiral binding with a pair of pliers, and then carefully twist the binding out to disassemble the notebook. Set the spiral binding, pages and back cover aside. Using a pencil and a ruler, mark in the diagonals on the notebook's front cover to find its exact centre. Pierce through this point with a dental pick or a needle.

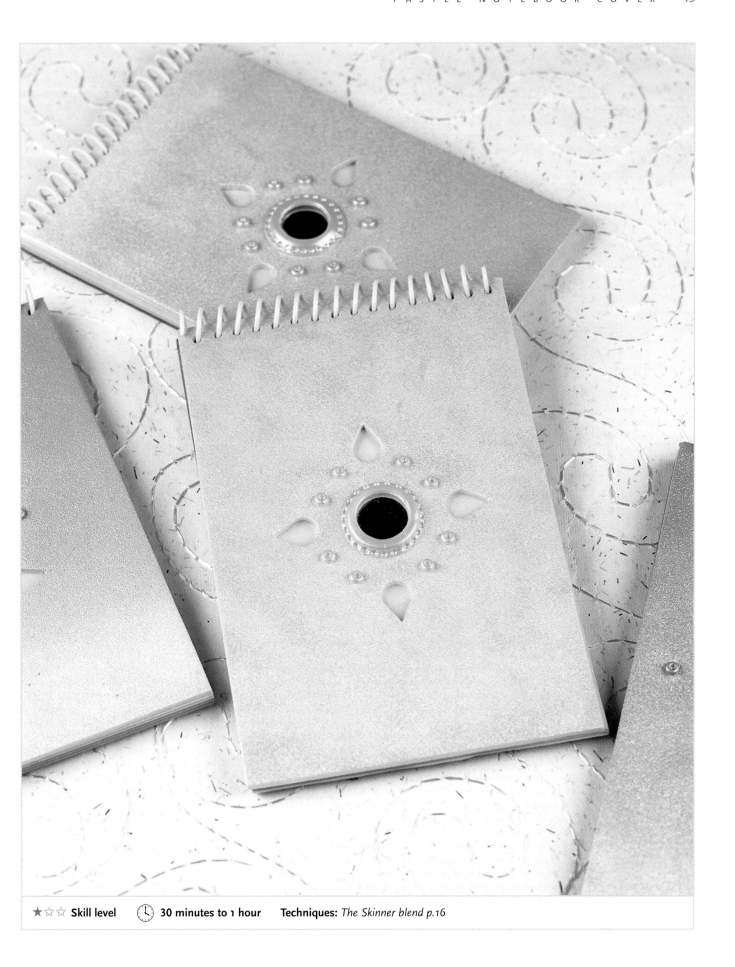

2 Use all of the white clay and an equal amount of yellow to form a Skinner blended sheet, following the instructions on page 16. Set the remaining yellow clay aside to be used later. Make the Skinner blend 2 mm ($^3/_{32}$ in) thick and large enough to accommodate the notebook cover. Smooth the blended clay on to the ceramic tile and press course sandpaper over the clay surface to texture.

3 Lay the cardboard cover over the clay. Using the blunt end of a wooden barbecue skewer, pierce through all of the holes at the top of the cover to make matching holes in the clay below. Piercing the holes will distort the flat clay surface a bit, and so, once all the holes have been made, roll once lightly over the cover with a hand roller to even out the clay below.

4 Cut around the cardboard cover with a tissue blade, trimming the clay below to the same shape. When all four sides are cut, carefully remove the surplus clay. Pierce through the pinhole in the cardboard cover with a dental pick or a pin to mark the centre point in the clay below. Carefully remove and discard the cardboard cover, leaving the clay cover in place on the tile.

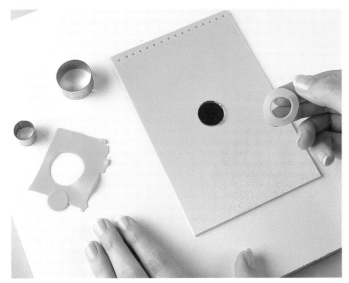

5 Roll a 1-mm (¹/₃₂-in)-thick sheet from the yellow clay and cut out a circle using the large round cutter. Use the smaller round cutter to cut a hole from the middle of the circle, making a round clay frame. Place the glass mirror in the middle of the clay cover, using the pin mark as a reference. Lay the clay frame over the mirror and push it down over the edge on to the clay below, securing the mirror in place.

6 Indent the outer edge of the clay frame with the ball stylus tool. (Do this to add decoration and to ensure that the frame is well joined to the clay cover below). Use the tear-drop cutter to cut four decorative holes into the clay cover as shown, and then carefully remove the cut out pieces with a dental pick or a needle, taking care not to distort the surrounding clay.

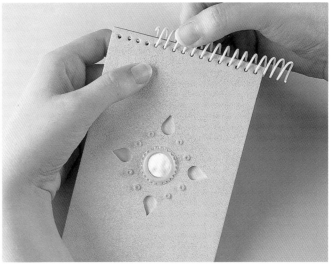

7 Roll or extrude the remaining scraps of yellow clay into a string 3 mm (¹/₈ in) in diameter. Cut eight sections from the string, each 3 mm (¹/₈ in) long, and roll each one between your fingertips to form a small ball. Place the balls between the holes on the cover. When happy with the positioning, push each ball into place with the ball stylus tool, attaching it firmly to the clay below.

8 Brush mica pigment powder all over the cover, then dust away the excess with a soft-bristled paintbrush. Bake the cover in place on the ceramic tile following the clay manufacturer's instructions. When cool, varnish the cover to protect the mica decoration. Once the varnish is dry, remove the cover from the tile and attach it to the notebook pages and back cover by re-inserting the spiral binding.

Sparkly quartz bird earrings

Tinted translucent polymer clay is used to make these pretty bird beads. Flakes of decorative metal leaf mixed into the clay shimmer below the surface, giving the clay the look of sparkling quartz. When finished with real gemstone beads and simple wire-working techniques, these birds are transformed into beautiful earrings to suit any occasion.

"When making the birds' eyes, be sure to use glass rhinestones, as plastic rhinestones may not withstand the heat of the baking process."

You will need

Materials

- ¼ block of translucent polymer clay
- large pinch of blue polymer clay
- Silver decorative metal leaf
- 2 glass rhinestones, 1 mm (¹/₃₂ in) in diameter
- Superglue
- Varnish
- 6 silver beads, 3 mm (¹/₈ in) in diameter
- 2 co-ordinating gemstone chip beads

- 2 silver headpins, at least 5 cm (2 in) in length
- 2 silver earring findings

Tools

- Metal ruler
- Tissue blade or craft knife
- 2 wooden toothpicks
- Wire mesh bead rack
- Wet/dry sandpaper
- Small jeweller's pliers
- Wire cutters

1 Colour the translucent clay with the blue clay, following the instructions on page 15. When the translucent clay is uniformly tinted, crumple up a sheet of silver decorative metal leaf and mix it into the clay. Knead or roll the clay well to break up the metal leaf and to mix it in completely.

2 Roll the sparkly translucent clay into a log 10 mm (³/₈ in) in diameter. Lay the log against a metal ruler and cut off two sections, each 4 cm (1½ in) long, using either a tissue blade or a craft knife. Roll each of the cut sections in turn between your palms to form two smooth, round balls.

3 Using your fingers, flatten each of the clay balls into a circular wafer shape. Continue finger-flattening the clay until each wafer is approximately 5 mm (³/₁₆ in) thick. There is no need to use a hand-roller to flatten the clay, as the surface does not need to be perfectly smooth, but do try to keep each wafer as close as possible to a true circle.

4 Fold each wafer in half. Pinch the folded-over clay together at the edges, working right around each seam in turn. Continue pinching the clay closer and closer together until you are able to smooth away the seams neatly and invisibly. Finger-smooth the surface of each piece so that the clay is free from any unsightly nicks or obvious fingerprints.

5 Pinch one corner of each piece, flattening out the clay slightly to make a short and stubby tail for each bird. Shape the clay gently between your fingers, stroking and smoothing it as you go, then use your finger to flatten each tail across the top, giving it a blunt end. Check that the pieces form a matching pair, and make any necessary adjustments.

6 Pinch the opposite corner of each piece outward to make the bird's neck and head. Carefully coax the clay out into a tapered point, extending a little way from the body, as shown. Repeat with the other clay piece, and check that the two form a matching pair. Finally, bend the tapered point over and down towards the body to make a stylized head for each bird.

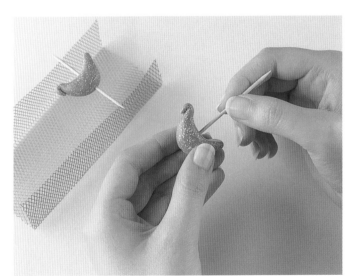

7 Give each bird a pair of eyes by pushing a glass rhinestone into the clay on either side of the head. Using the wooden toothpicks, pierce a hole vertically through the middle of each bird, and then suspend the bird beads on a bead rack, ready for baking. Bake the beads in place on the rack, following the clay manufacturer's recommendations, and allow them to cool completely.

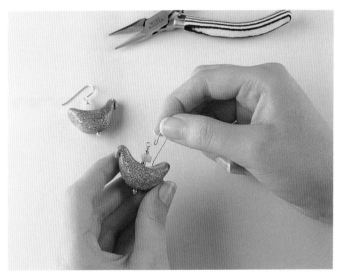

8 Remove the rhinestones and wet-sand the bird beads smooth. When dry, superglue the rhinestones back into place and then varnish the beads. When the varnish has dried, thread the bird beads, the silver beads and the gemstone chips on to the headpins, as shown. Finish each headpin by turning a wrapped loop, following the directions on page 22, and then attach the earring findings.

Millefiore charm bracelet

Never out of fashion, charm bracelets are easy to make using colourful millefiore canes. The directions below will make a bracelet of around 20 cm (8 in) in length. This is a little larger than average, but it will allow the bracelet to hang loosely on the wrist. For a smaller bracelet, use a shorter chain with fewer charms.

"Make your own millefiore canes for this project following the directions on page 18, or buy ready-made canes from craft stores or over the Internet."

You will need

Materials

- 3 co-ordinating millefiore canes, each 5 cm (2 in) long and 15 mm (5/8 in) in diameter
- 16 silver top pins
- Polymer clay to match the outside colour of each cane; allow 1/8 block per cane
- Superglue
- 19-cm (7-in) length of large-linked silver chain
- 16 silver jump rings, 5 mm (3/16 in) in diameter
- Silver bracelet clasp

Tools

- Metal ruler
- Sharp tissue blade
- Baking tray, lined with baking parchment
- Non-flammable polyester batting
- 2 pairs of jeweller's pliers

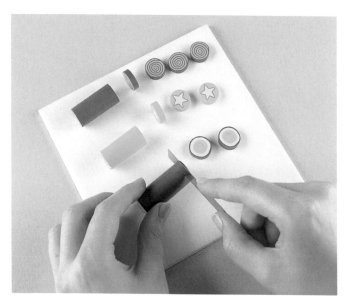

1 Select three co-ordinating millefiore canes, each reduced to a diameter of 15 mm (5/8 in). Using a sharp tissue blade, cut slices 3 mm (1/8 in) thick from the canes. Cut four slices from your favourite cane and three slices from each of the other two to make ten slices overall. Set the remainder of each cane aside to be used later in the project.

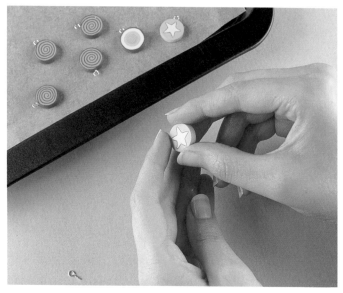

2 Soften the harsh edges of the cane slices by stroking them gently with your fingertips. Push a top pin into the edge of each slice, keeping the loop facing forwards. Lay the finished cane slice charms flat on a baking tray lined with baking parchment, ready for baking.

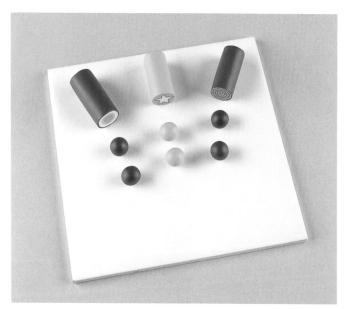

3 Make bases for the six ball charms. For each cane, roll two 10-mm (³/₈-in) balls using clay that matches the cane's outside colour. For the canes pictured, this will be orange balls for the star cane and purple balls for each of the other two. Matching the base colour to the cane ensures that any gaps between the cane slices applied later will not be noticeable.

4 Reduce the leftover canes to 8 mm (⁵/₁₆ in) in diameter and cut slices 1 mm (¹/₃₂ in) thick from each. Cover each ball with cane slices of the appropriate colour, making two ball charms from each cane. Roll the balls smooth and then insert a top pin into each one. Place the ball charms on some polyester batting and set on a baking tray, ready for baking.

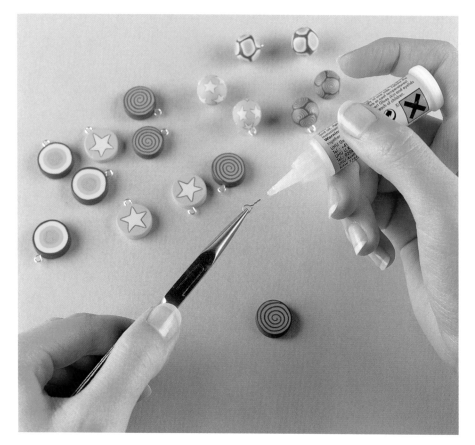

5 Bake all the charms following the clay manufacturer's recommendations, and then allow them to cool. Taking each charm in turn, remove the top pin with a pair of pliers and glue it back into place with a drop of superglue. This will keep the pins securely embedded in the charms. Make sure you keep the loops facing forwards on the cane-slice charms.

Helpful hint
Take great care when using superglue, as it can bond your skin to anything and everything in seconds.

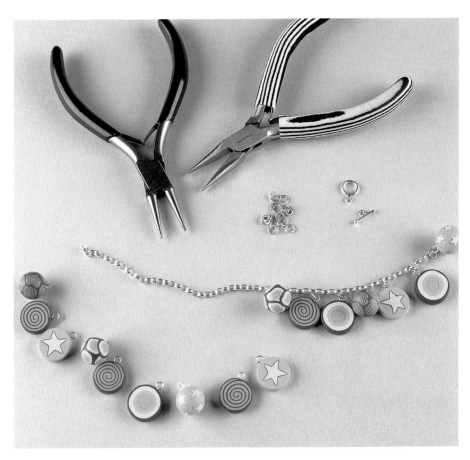

6 Arrange the charms against the silver chain. Look for natural repeats in the chain and, using a ruler, try to space the charms every 12 mm (½ in) or so. When you are happy with the arrangement, fix the charms to the chain with jump rings, using a pair of pliers in each hand to twist the jump rings open and closed. Attach the clasp to the finished bracelet.

Variation

Matching earrings

Add a few charms to short lengths of chain. Hang them from earring wires to make earrings to match this fun, colourful bracelet.

Terracotta treasures

Breathe new life into terracotta flowerpots with these easily sculpted vegetables, typical of a kitchen garden. Keep the finished flowerpots indoors to protect the decoration from the elements. Use them in the conservatory or sun lounge, or for growing herbs along the kitchen window ledge.

"You can easily adapt this project to create other adornments, using your favourite vegetables as inspiration."

You will need

Materials

- Terracotta flowerpot, 11 cm (4 in) in diameter
- PVA glue
- ½ block of teal polymer clay
- ¼ block of pale green polymer clay
- ½ block of leaf green polymer clay
- ¼ block of orange polymer clay
- ¼ block of red polymer clay
- ¼ block of white polymer clay
- Purple decorating chalk

Tools

- Pasta machine or hand roller
- Metal ruler
- Craft knife
- Star cutter, 10 mm (³⁄₈ in) in diameter
- Leaf cutter, 20 mm (³⁄₄ in) in diameter
- Tissue blade
- Paintbrush
- Ceramic tile (optional)

1 Coat the flowerpot rim with PVA glue. Roll the teal clay into a long strip, a little wider than the rim and 1.5 mm (¹⁄₁₆ in) thick. Wrap the strip around the rim and trim where it overlaps. Butt the cut edges together and smooth away the seam. Fold the top of the strip over inside the pot, then trim around the inside edge with a craft knife.

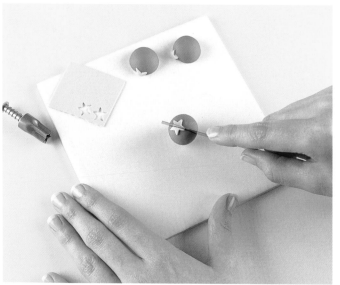

2 Roll two red balls 20 mm (³⁄₄ in) in diameter to make the tomatoes. Roll a pale green sheet 1.5 mm (¹⁄₁₆ in) thick and cut out two stars with the star cutter to form the calyxes. Set the remainder of the sheet aside. Place a calyx on the top of each tomato, then cut the tomatoes in half with a tissue blade, cutting through the calyxes.

★★☆ **Skill level**   ⏱ **1-2 hours**   **Techniques:** *Rolling and piercing balls p.14, Wrapping and cutting seams p.14*

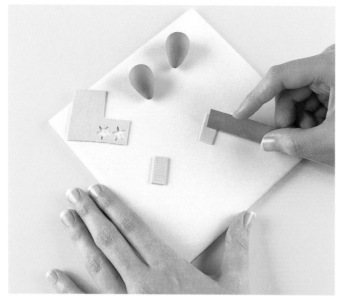

3 Roll two orange balls 20 mm (³⁄₄ in) in diameter and taper them into cones to make the carrots. Cut two rectangles measuring 10 mm (³⁄₈ in) by 20 mm (³⁄₄ in) from the leftover pale green sheet. Use a tissue blade to cut lines like the teeth of a comb along one side of each rectangle, turning the rectangles into small fringes.

4 Roll up the clay fringes to make leaves for the carrots. Using the handle of a paintbrush, make a hole in the top of each carrot and insert the rolled-up leaves. Carefully cut each carrot in half, cutting through the leaves at the top so that each half has equal leaves. Use the tissue blade to indent horizontal markings on each carrot half.

5 Roll two 20-mm (³⁄₄-in) white balls to make the turnips. Taper each ball into a cone, making it shorter and fatter than the carrots. Make and insert the leaves as before, then cut each turnip in half. Indent horizontal lines across each turnip half with the tissue blade, then brush the top half of each turnip with purple decorating chalk to colour.

6 Roll two leaf green balls 12 mm (¹⁄₂ in) in diameter. Taper each ball into a cigar shape and then flatten slightly to make the pea pod shells. Roll four pale green balls, around 6 mm (¹⁄₄ in) in diameter, to make the peas. Sandwich the peas between the shells, pinching the clay together at the back to secure, and repeat to make four pods in total.

7 Roll the remaining leaf green clay into a sheet 1.5 mm (¹⁄₁₆ in) thick. Working on a ceramic tile or other smooth work surface, cut out several leaves using the leaf cutter. Re-roll the surplus clay to cut more leaves if necessary. Loosen the leaves from the tile or work surface by sliding a tissue blade carefully underneath the clay.

8 Arrange the vegetables and leaves around the flowerpot rim. Push them lightly on to the clay to begin with, so you can lift and reposition individual pieces if necessary. When happy with the arrangement, push each vegetable into place as firmly as you can without distorting the clay, and bake according to the clay manufacturer's recommendations.

Variation

Family favourites

There is no need to stick to the vegetables shown in the main project. You can decorate your flowerpot using any vegetables you like – ask your family members what their favourites are and adorn your flowerpot accordingly! The flowerpot shown here was made using the same techniques as in the main project, but it has been adapted slightly to feature eggplants, red peppers, corn and pumpkins.

Scrapbooking embellishments

Scrapbooking, the tradition of creatively displaying photographs, has made a welcome comeback in the last few years. Here, we make a variety of baby-themed embellishments to adorn a scrapbook page. You can easily adapt these ideas to make embellishments with other themes, too.

"Baked polymer clay is acid- and lignin-free, so it will not adversely affect photographs."

You will need

Materials

- Pale blue and white striped millefiore cane
- ½ block of pale blue polymer clay
- ½ block of peach polymer clay
- ¼ block of pink polymer clay
- ¼ block of pale yellow polymer clay
- Pinch of white polymer clay
- 6 silver top pins
- Wet/dry sandpaper
- Assortment of coloured paper or cardstock for mounting the photographs
- Embroidery yarn, about 20 cm (8 in) in length
- PVA glue
- Scrapbook paper, 30 x 30 cm (12 x 12 in)
- Assortment of photographs

- Superglue
- Double-sided adhesive tape (optional)

Tools

- Pasta machine or hand roller
- 4 ceramic tiles
- Baby bodysuit, sock and mitten templates (see page 93), traced and cut out
- Tissue blade
- Craft knife
- Jeweller's pliers
- Dental pick or needle
- Flower cutter, 3 cm (1¼ in) in diameter
- Ball stylus tool
- "1" "2" and "3" number cutters, 4 cm (1½ in) long
- "A" "B" and "C" alphabet cutters, 3 cm (1¼ in) long

1 Using a pasta machine or a hand roller, roll a blue sheet 1 mm (¹⁄₃₂ in) thick and large enough to accommodate the baby bodysuit template. Cover with thin slices cut lengthways from the striped cane. With the stripes running vertically, roll the sheet out to 2 mm (³⁄₃₂ in) thick to smooth the cane slices together. Lay the striped sheet on a ceramic tile with the stripes running horizontally.

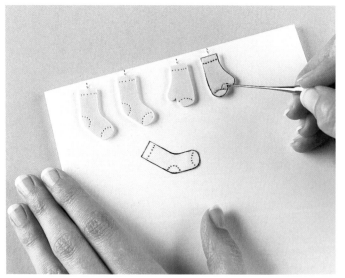

2 Cut a baby bodysuit from the striped sheet, cutting around the template with a tissue blade. Place three tiny white clay balls along the bottom to make the poppers, and edge the collar and cuffs with fine white clay string. Use pliers to hold and push a top pin into each shoulder, ensuring the loops face sideways. Leave the baby bodysuit on a tile, ready for baking.

3 Roll yellow and pink sheets, each 2 mm ($^3/_{32}$ in) thick, and lay them on one of the tiles. Using the sock template and a craft knife, cut two yellow socks. Cut a pink mitten, then flip the template over to cut the second, so that the thumbs are on opposite sides. Insert top pins as before and prick through the templates with a dental pick or needle to add the stitching details.

4 Roll the peach, pink and remaining blue clay into sheets 1.5 mm ($^1/_{16}$ in) thick. Working on a new ceramic tile, cut two flowers from each colour using the flower cutter and set the remaining sheets aside. Form six yellow balls 8 mm ($^5/_{16}$ in) in diameter and flatten them slightly. Lay a ball on the centre of each flower and indent it with a ball stylus tool to add texture.

5 Roll a yellow clay sheet 1.5 mm ($^1/_{16}$ in) thick. Working on a ceramic tile, cut the numbers 1, 2 and 3 from the yellow, blue and peach sheets, respectively. To make a background for the alphabet blocks, cut three squares large enough to accommodate the letters from the peach sheet. Cut an A, B and C from the blue, pink and yellow sheets and place a letter on each peach square.

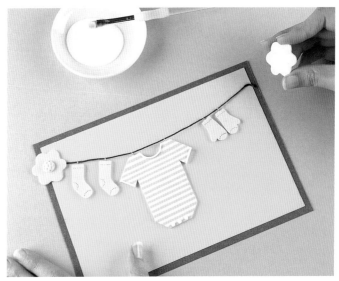

6 Bake all the clay embellishments on their tiles, following the clay manufacturer's recommendations. When cool, remove the top pins from the baby clothes, using pliers for ease. Wet-sand the edges of all the embellishments, as shown, to smooth away any rough areas. Dry the pieces and glue the top pins back into place with superglue, taking care to keep the loops facing sideways.

7 Make a paper or cardstock backing to display the clothesline. Thread the baby clothes on to a length of embroidery yarn and glue the yarn ends to either side of the backing with PVA glue. Glue a baked flower over the yarn ends. When the glue has dried and the line is secure, arrange the clothing along the line and glue each item down to the backing.

8 Prepare any photos you wish to use, mounting or framing them with coloured cardstock or paper. Arrange the photos, the clothes line montage and the other embellishments over the scrapbook paper. Experiment with different layouts and, when you are happy, secure each item down into place with PVA glue or doubled-sided adhesive tape.

Little princess photo frame

What a great way to display photos of any princesses in your family. These nifty polka-dot frames are just right for a passport or a wallet-sized photograph. The magnet on the back allows them to take pride of place on the refrigerator – where all good works of art belong!

"Be sure to trace the templates for this project rather than photocopying them, so you can see through the template when positioning it on the clay."

You will need

Materials

- 1 block of lilac polymer clay
- 1/8 block of gold polymer clay
- 1/16 block of white polymer clay
- Metric 1-cm graph paper (or Imperial 1/8-inch graph paper)
- Photo-frame templates (front, back and wall, see page 93), traced and cut out
- Wet/dry sandpaper
- Superglue
- Magnet
- Favourite photo

Tools

- Pasta machine (optional)
- Hand roller
- 2 ceramic tiles
- Craft knife
- Tissue blade
- Dental pick or needle
- Ball stylus tool
- Extruder (optional)

1 Roll half of the lilac clay into a sheet 2 mm (3/32 in) thick and lay the sheet on a tile. Use a tissue blade to trim the sheet so it just accommodates the frame front template. Lay a piece of graph paper diagonally over the clay and use a dental pick or needle to prick through the paper, marking every 1 cm (3/8 in) to form a grid of pin-pricks in the clay beneath.

2 Remove the graph paper and indent a small hollow over all the pinpricks, using a ball-stylus tool. Roll or extrude a thin string of white clay 2 mm (³⁄₃₂ in) thick. Cut tiny 1-mm (¹⁄₃₂-in) sections from the string and roll them into balls with your fingertips. Place the tiny white balls into the hollows on the sheet to form a polka-dot pattern.

3 Roll the clay gently with a hand roller until the white balls have sunk in and the clay is smooth. Lay the frame front template over the sheet, looking through the tracing paper to find the best position, and cut around the template with a craft knife. Remove the surplus clay, leaving the frame front in place on the tile.

4 Roll a gold clay log 5 mm (³⁄₁₆ in) in diameter. Cut two sections 15 mm (⁵⁄₈ in) long and roll into tapered logs. Coil up the ends to make two "S"-shaped scrolls and place them above the frame's aperture. Cut five more sections 5 mm (³⁄₁₆ in) long each and roll them into balls. Flatten the balls slightly with your fingertips and place one on each of the crown's points.

5 Roll the remaining lilac clay into a sheet 2 mm (³⁄₃₂ in) thick, and lay it on another tile. Lay the frame back template over the clay and cut around it with a tissue blade. Cut out three thin rectangles using the frame wall template and remove the surplus clay. Place the three walls on to the frame back, running them parallel to the bottom and side edges as shown.

6 Bake the frame parts in place on the tiles, following the clay manufacturer's recommendations, and allow them to cool completely. Wet-sand the edges of the frame front to neaten, and then allow the clay to dry. Glue the front and the back of the frame together with superglue, ensuring that the open edge on the frame's back is at the top.

7 Glue the magnet to the back of the frame with superglue. When the glue has dried, drop a favourite photograph into the frame and use it to brighten up the refrigerator door or any other metal surface.

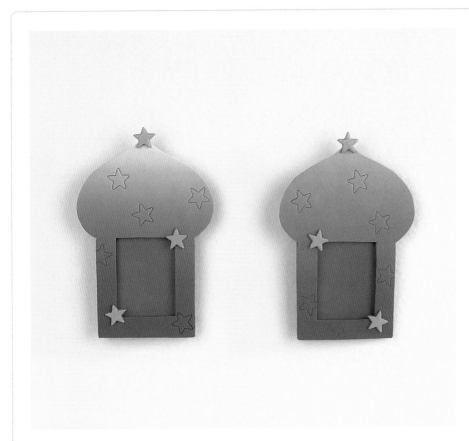

Variation

Blended minaret frames

Inspired by exotic buildings with minarets, these frames were made using blended clay, then impressed with a star cutter. See page 93 for a template for these frames.

Mokume gane trinket box

Trinket boxes are great for hiding jewellery and other small keepsakes – and they make superb gifts, too! These mokume gane trinket boxes are easy to make using a metal cookie cutter as a former. With so many different cutters available, you can make these boxes in whatever shape or size you wish.

"Any colour combination is possible when making these special boxes. Why not make one to match your bedroom or your bathroom décor?"

You will need

Materials

- 1½ blocks of lilac polymer clay
- ½ block of purple polymer clay
- Pink translucent mokume gane slab (see page 16 for instructions)
- Purple translucent mokume gane slab (see page 16 for instructions)
- Liquid polymer clay
- Varnish
- 8-cm (3⅛-in) copper wire, 1-mm diameter (18-gauge)
- Focal bead 20 mm (¾ in) in diameter (the hole must be able to accommodate the copper wire)
- 6 assorted seed beads (with holes that will accommodate the copper wire)
- Superglue

Tools

- Pasta machine (optional)
- Round cookie cutter, 7 cm (2¾ in) in diameter
- Tissue blade
- Hand roller
- Craft knife
- Wet/dry sandpaper
- Soft-bristled paintbrush
- 2 ceramic tiles
- Extruder
- Jeweller's chain-nosed pliers
- Wire cutters
- Small drill-bit, 1 mm (¹/₃₂ in) in diameter

1 Roll a strip of lilac clay 2 mm (³/₃₂ in) thick. Make it long enough to wrap around the cookie cutter and a little wider than the cutter is tall. Cover the strip with thin slices of pink mokume gane clay, cut from the slab with a tissue blade. When the strip is completely covered, roll over it lightly with a hand roller to smooth away the seams between the mokume gane slices, then trim the edges to neaten.

★★★ **Skill level**   🕐 **1-2 hours**   **Techniques:** *Wrapping and cutting seams p.14, Mokume gane p.16*

2 Wrap the strip around the cookie cutter to make the wall section for the box, cutting the strip where it overlaps and butting the cut edges together neatly. Trim the clay in line with the top of the cutter. Bake the clay, in place on the cutter, following the clay manufacturer's recommendations. When cool, slide the wall section from the cutter and wet-sand it smooth. Apply a coat of varnish and allow the varnish to dry.

3 To make the box lid, roll a lilac clay sheet 2 mm (³/₃₂ in) thick and large enough to accommodate the wall section. Cover the sheet with slices cut from the purple mokume gane slab and roll smooth as before. Lay the sheet upside down on a ceramic tile. Place the wall section on the clay and cut around it with a craft knife. Set the wall section aside and remove the surplus clay, leaving just the upside-down lid in place on the tile.

4 Fit the extruder with the 3-mm (¹/₈-in) round-holed die and extrude some purple clay. Edge the lid with the extruded clay string, cutting it where it overlaps and butting the cut edges together. To make the flange, roll a purple clay sheet 2 mm (³/₃₂ in) thick and large enough to accommodate the wall section. Set the wall section on the sheet and cut around the inside edge. Place the resulting clay circle centrally on the upside-down lid and smooth it down.

5 To make the base of the box, roll a lilac clay sheet 2 mm (³/₃₂ in) thick and large enough to accommodate the wall section. Smooth the sheet onto the second ceramic tile. Dot a little liquid polymer clay around the bottom edge of the wall section, then place it on to the sheet. Cut around the outside of the wall section with a craft knife, this time leaving it in place when you have finished, and remove the surplus clay.

6 Extrude more purple clay string and wrap it around the bottom of the box to hide the cut clay. Cut the string where it overlaps and butt the cut edges together neatly. Bake the box and lid in place on their respective ceramic tiles, following the clay manufacturer's recommendations. When the baked pieces are cool, remove them from the tiles. Wet-sand the box lid smooth and then varnish with a soft-bristled paintbrush, allowing the varnish to dry completely.

7 Thread the focal bead and seed beads on to the copper wire to make a handle. To make short legs, bend the wire down at right angles on either side of the beads using the chain-nosed pliers. Trim the legs to 12 mm (¹/₂ in) long using wire cutters. Determine where on the box lid to place the handle and, twisting the drill-bit between your fingers, hand-drill tiny holes in the lid to accommodate the wire legs. Attach the handle by gluing the legs into the holes using superglue.

Variation

Mokume gane bead necklace

Rather than mixing your leftover translucent mokume gane scraps into your usual scrap pile, use it to make beautiful beads, as shown here. Before long, you will have enough beads to make a very attractive necklace.

Faux enamelled bracelet

Add wonderful enamelled effects to jewellery projects with colourful epoxy resins (cold enamels). For this two-toned bracelet, be sure to choose epoxy resins with translucent colours rather than opaque, as the former will allow the distressed silver effects to show through.

"Remember that most epoxy resins take 24 hours to harden completely, so if you are making this bracelet as a gift, be sure to plan ahead and leave enough setting time."

You will need

Materials

- ½ block of silver polymer clay
- Silver decorative metal leaf
- PVA glue (optional)
- 10 silver top pins
- Superglue
- Varnish
- Translucent blue and green epoxy resins
- Liquid hardener for epoxy resins
- 6 silver jump rings, 5 mm (³/₁₆ in) in diameter
- Silver bracelet clasp

Tools

- Pasta machine or hand roller
- Round cutter, 25 mm (1 in) in diameter
- Extruder (optional)
- Tissue blade or craft knife
- Flat soft-bristled paintbrush
- Clay modelling tool
- Ceramic tile
- Jeweller's pliers
- Flat stiff-bristled paintbrush
- Mixing cups
- 2 wooden toothpicks
- Protective gloves

1 Roll the silver clay into a sheet 4 mm (⁵/₃₂ in) thick, and cut five circles with the round cutter to make the bracelet links. Note that most pasta machines cannot roll the clay thick enough, so if you wish to use the machine, form a sheet 2 mm (³/₃₂ in) thick and fold it in half to double the thickness.

2 Fill the extruder with the surplus silver clay. Using a 6-mm (¼-in) slit die, extrude the clay into a long ribbon. Cut the ribbon into five sections, each long enough to wrap around the round cutter with a small overlap. If you do not have an extruder, roll a silver sheet 1 mm (¹/₃₂ in) thick, and cut suitable strips 6 mm (¼ in) wide.

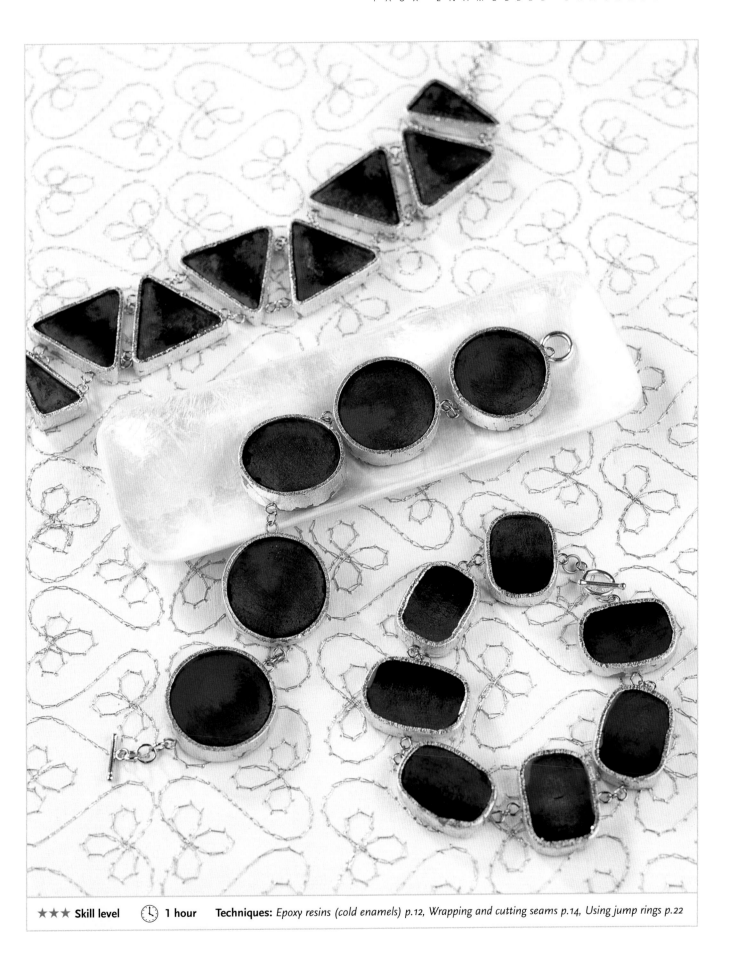

★★★ **Skill level**   🕐 **1 hour**   **Techniques:** *Epoxy resins (cold enamels) p.12, Wrapping and cutting seams p.14, Using jump rings p.22*

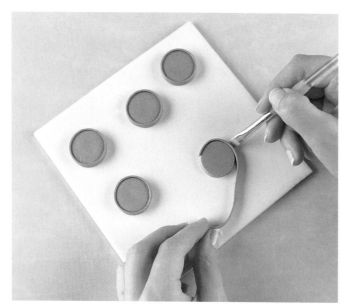

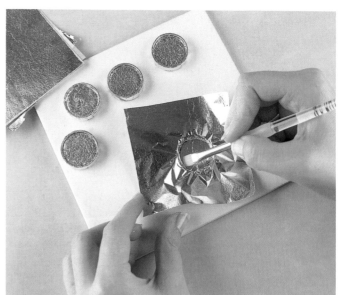

3 Use a flat soft-bristled paintbrush to push a clay ribbon around the edge of each link, making a wall to hold in the resin. Cut the ribbon where it overlaps and butt the cut edges together neatly. Smooth the seam very carefully with a clay modelling tool, ensuring the cut edges are well joined, but taking care not to distort the clay wall.

4 Cover each link with decorative metal leaf. Carefully push the leaf on to the clay with the soft-bristled paintbrush, starting in the middle and working outwards and down over the sides. For stubborn areas, you can use a smear of PVA glue and add more leaf, although letting the duller clay show in areas does give a pleasing aged effect.

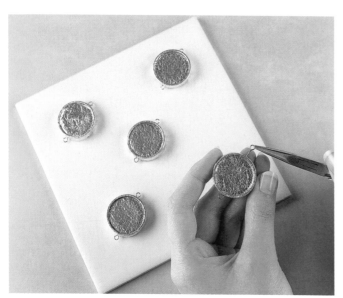

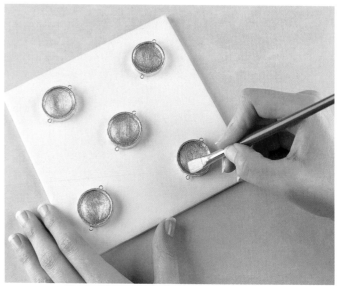

5 Push two top pins into the base of each link, placing them opposite each other so the links can be joined together (for greater ease, use a small pair of jeweller's pliers to hold the pins). Set the links on to a ceramic tile, ready for baking. Firmly smooth the links down on to the tile to ensure that they bake flat, but take care not to distort the delicate sides.

6 Lightly scratch inside each link with a flat, stiff-bristled paintbrush. This makes the metal leaf more reflective so that the epoxy resins will be more dazzling. Bake the links, following the clay manufacturer's recommendations, then varnish to protect the metal leaf. When the varnish is dry, remove the top pins and superglue them back into place.

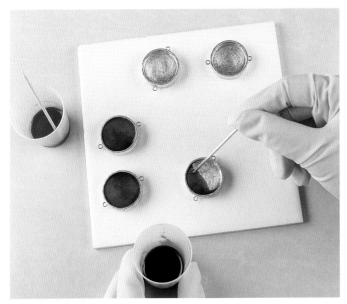

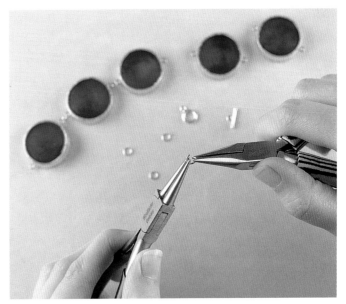

7 Wearing protective gloves, prepare the blue and green epoxy resins, following the manufacturer's directions. Use a wooden toothpick to scoop up the resin, drop by drop, and fill half of each link with blue resin and the other half with green. Coax the resin into the edges and slightly blend the colours together in the middle to form a smooth gradation.

8 Set the links aside for 24 hours to allow the epoxy resin to harden completely. Keep the links totally flat and under cover so the epoxy sets level and is protected from falling dust – a shelf inside a display cabinet is ideal. When the resins have hardened completely, join the links together with 5-mm (3/16-in) jump rings and attach a silver bracelet clasp.

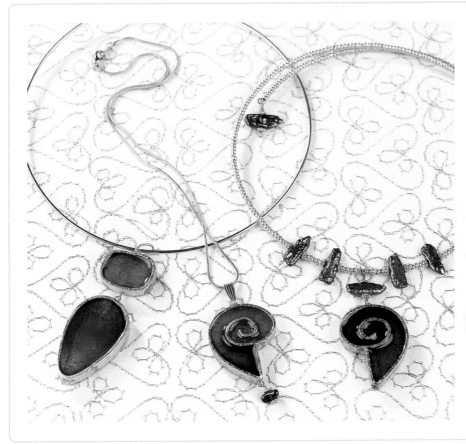

Variation

Gold-toned enamelled pendants

Gold decorative leaf can be just as attractive as silver, as this collection of faux enamelled pendants shows. Remember to use gold polymer clay when using gold leaf.

Mosaic picture frame

You can make and bake all kinds of polymer clay mosaic tiles to embed into unbaked clay, or to glue to finished projects. The tiles on this frame are laid into position before baking, creating a quick and easy one-bake project. Choose a wooden frame with wide, flat borders for this project.

"This frame is perfect for displaying your treasured family portraits."

You will need

Materials

- Wooden picture frame, 21 x 26 cm (8 x 10 in)
- PVA glue
- 1 block of emerald green polymer clay
- 1¼ blocks of white polymer clay
- ¼ block of blue polymer clay
- ¼ block of bright green polymer clay
- ¼ block of teal polymer clay
- ¼ block of turquoise polymer clay
- ¼ block of purple polymer clay
- Clingfilm
- Talcum powder (optional)

Tools

- Soft-bristled paintbrush
- Pasta machine or hand roller
- Metal ruler
- 5 ceramic tiles
- Permanent ink pen
- Heart cutter, 4 cm (1½ in) in diameter
- Tissue blade
- Craft knife

1 Remove the glass and backing from the frame. Using a soft-bristled paintbrush, paint the border and side edges with a thin, unbroken coat of PVA glue and allow the glue to dry completely. The glue will help the clay adhere to the frame, and will also seal the wood, providing a barrier against any remaining sap or preservatives that might seep out and mar the clay.

2 Roll the emerald clay into strips 1 mm (¹⁄₃₂ in) thick, and wide enough to cover the frame's border and sides. Smooth the strips on to the border and down over the sides, then trim off any excess clay from the back of the frame. Continue adding clay strips, butting them together neatly. When the frame is completely covered, smooth all the seams.

★★★ **Skill level**   🕐 **1-2 hours**   **Techniques:** *Marbling p.15*

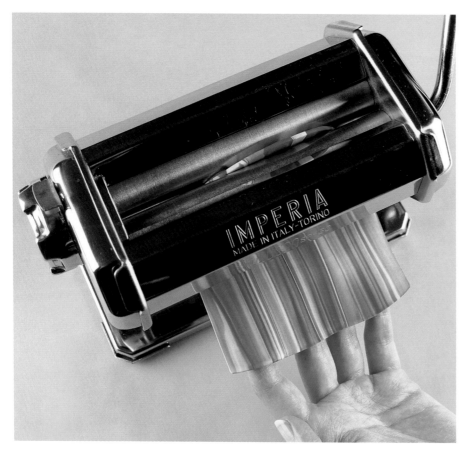

3 Marble together a ¼-block section of white clay with the blue clay, following the directions on page 15. Flatten the marbled clay into a patty, then roll it out into a sheet 2 mm (³/₃₂ in) thick. Repeat with the remaining colours, marbling each different colour with a ¼ block of white to form turquoise, bright green, teal and purple marbled sheets.

4 The mosaic tiles should fit the frame neatly, with a small gap between each tile. I used 2-cm (³/₄-in) tiles, but make whatever size tile works best with your frame. To make cutting guides, measure and mark along the sides of four ceramic tiles, making a mark with a permanent ink pen every 2 cm (³/₄ in), or whichever interval matches the length of the tiles you need.

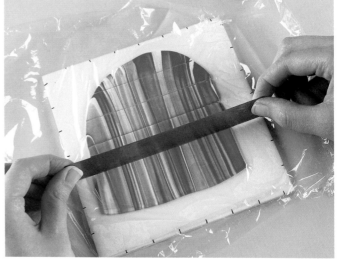

5 Lay the blue marbled sheet on to one of the marked ceramic tiles. Smooth some clingfilm over the clay to bevel the edges as you cut and push down into the clay with a tissue blade, aligning it with the guide marks to cut a grid of mosaic tiles. Using separate ceramic tiles, repeat with the bright green, teal and turquoise marbled clay, but leave the purple marbled sheet uncut.

6 Lay the purple marbled sheet on to a ceramic tile and cover it with clingfilm. Using the heart-shaped cutter, cut out three purple hearts and remove the surplus clay. Slide a tissue blade underneath each heart to loosen it from the tile with the least possible distortion. If the blade sticks to the clay, dust it with a little talcum powder to reduce the drag.

7 Loosen all the clay mosaic tiles by sliding a tissue blade underneath the clay as before. Carefully place the tiles randomly over the picture frame, leaving a small gap between each one. Lay the tiles down lightly at first so you can easily lift and reposition them if necessary; push them down more firmly once you are happy with the arrangement.

8 Choose an area of the frame to site the heart motifs. Cover with clingfilm and push the cutter gently into the clay, aiming to cut just the tiles and not the emerald clay base. Carefully pick out the cut tiles with a craft knife and fit the purple clay heart into the hole. Repeat for the remaining two hearts. Bake the frame, following the clay manufacturer's instructions.

Croissant bead eyeglass leash

This stylish eyeglass leash features croissant beads, a polymer clay version of the popular rolled-up paper beads. They are teamed with silver, glass and freshwater pearl beads to make a leash of around 74 cm (29 in) in length. If the leash were any longer, the spectacle lenses might get scratched by a belt buckle or a zip. Bear this in mind if you decide to design your own leash, and always keep an eye on the overall length.

"Many people wear spectacles or sunglasses, so these eyeglass leashes make great gifts, too!"

You will need

Materials

- ¼ block of purple polymer clay
- ¼ block of lilac polymer clay
- Silver decorative metal leaf
- Talcum powder
- Mica pigment powder, duo red/blue colour
- Varnish
- 85-cm (33-in) length of tigertail
- 2 crimps
- 2 rubber eyeglass leash findings
- 5-10 g, copper-coloured glass seed beads, size 8
- 42 silver daisy spacer beads, 4 mm (⁵/₃₂ in) in diameter
- 11 white freshwater pearl beads, 5 mm (³/₁₆ in) in diameter

Tools

- Pasta machine or hand roller
- 2 ceramic tiles
- Large and small soft-bristled paintbrushes
- Tissue blade
- Croissant bead templates (see page 93), traced and cut out
- 10 wooden toothpicks
- Wire-mesh bead rack (see page 21)
- Baking tray
- Jeweller's chain-nosed pliers or crimping pliers

1 Roll the purple clay into a sheet 1 mm (¹/₃₂ in) thick and lay it on a ceramic tile. Roll the lilac clay into a 2-mm (³/₃₂-in)-thick sheet and cover it with silver decorative metal leaf, smoothing the leaf down with a large soft-bristled paintbrush. Crackle the leaf by rolling the lilac sheet thinner until it reaches 1 mm (¹/₃₂ in) thick, and then lay it on a separate ceramic tile.

2 Using a tissue blade, cut ten large triangles from the purple sheet, cutting around the large croissant bead template. Leave the triangles in place on the tile and remove the surplus clay. Using the smaller bead template, cut ten triangles from the silver-leafed lilac sheet, again leaving them in place on the tile and removing the surplus clay.

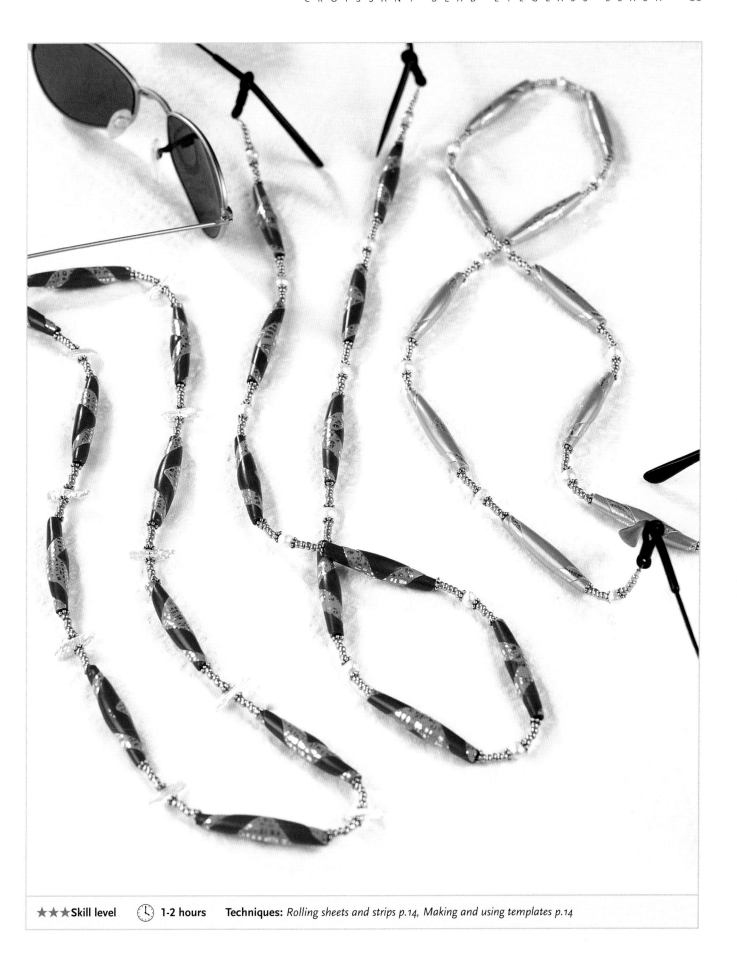

★★★Skill level   🕐 1-2 hours   **Techniques:** *Rolling sheets and strips p.14, Making and using templates p.14*

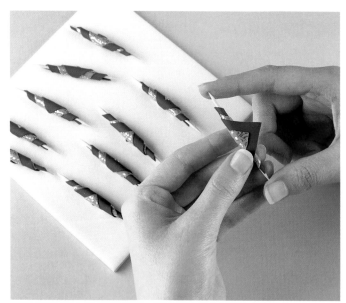

3 Carefully slide a tissue blade underneath all the triangles to free them from the tiles with as little distortion as possible. Place the smaller triangles on top of the larger ones as shown, aligning the two together at their bases. Smooth the triangles together with your fingertips to ensure they are firmly attached and to expel any trapped air.

4 Dust the wooden toothpicks with talcum powder. Take each pair of triangles in turn and wrap them around a toothpick, rolling the clay up like a pastry croissant. Roll the clay as tightly as you can. This can take a bit of practice, but don't worry if the beads are not perfect, as their shape will be refined in the next step.

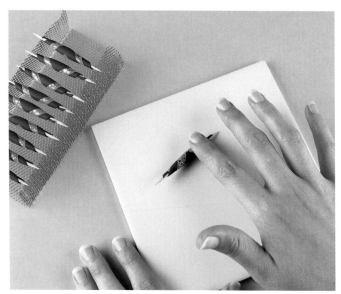

5 Shape the beads into smooth bicones. Rest your index finger on each bead in turn and roll the bead back and forth along the work surface to soften its shape. Use a very light pressure and keep your finger moving up and down the length of the bead as you roll. When smooth, place the bead aside on the wire mesh bead rack.

6 Keep the beads on the toothpicks and trim their ends to a neat line with a tissue blade, taking care to keep the blade well away from your fingers! Loosen the beads so they turn freely on the toothpicks, and set them back on the bead rack. If you push any of the beads out of shape while trimming, just carefully roll them back into shape as before.

7 Dust all of the beads with the mica pigment powder. Return the beads to the bead rack and place the rack on to a baking tray. Bake the beads according to the clay manufacturer's recommendations and allow them to cool completely before handling. Finally, give each bead a coat of varnish to protect and enhance the mica powder and allow the varnish to dry.

8 Thread a crimp and a leash finding on to the tigertail. Bring the end of the tigertail back through the crimp and then squash the crimp to secure the finding in place. Thread the beads following the pattern shown and finish with another crimp and leash finding, securing as before. Thread the remnants of tigertail back through the beads to hide.

Variation

Croissant bead watches

These elegant dress watches are threaded with different variations of croissant beads. Try rolling up triangles of different sizes, cutting the beads in half or flattening the beads after rolling for an array of different effects.

Klimt-inspired bottle

A simple glass bottle is brought to life in this project, inspired by the work of Gustav Klimt. This Viennese artist adored colour and pattern and would often use real gold leaf in his paintings. I am sure that if he were alive today, he would be enjoying the colourful possibilities of polymer clay art!

"The quantities below are enough to embellish a medium-sized bottle. Adjust the amounts accordingly for larger or smaller bottles."

You will need

Materials

- 1 block of pink polymer clay
- ½ block of pale blue polymer clay
- Polymer clay to make the canes, allow nine different colours, 1/16 block per colour
- Coloured glass bottle, 18 cm (7 in) tall x 4 cm (1½ in) wide.
- Gold and silver decorative metal leaf
- PVA glue
- Varnish
- Graph paper (optional)

Tools

- Hand roller
- Pasta machine (optional)
- Craft knife
- metal ruler
- Large soft-bristled paintbrush
- Extruder
- Tissue blade
- Paintbrushes for gluing and varnishing
- Non-flammable polyester batting

1 Roll the pink clay into a sheet 1.5 mm (1/16 in) thick. Cut out a rectangle 5 cm (2 in) wide and long enough to wrap around the bottle. Use a craft knife and metal ruler to cut the rectangle or to make a graph paper template to cut around. Use the surplus clay to make a second rectangle of the same length and thickness, but this one should be only 3 cm (1¼ in) wide.

2 Cover the large rectangle with gold-coloured decorative metal leaf. Lay the metal leaf directly on to the clay and smooth it down with a soft brush. Work along the rectangle, adding metal leaf until the clay is completely covered and neatly trim away any overhanging leaf. Repeat to cover the smaller rectangle with silver-coloured decorative metal leaf.

3 Make three different extruded canes, using the extruder fitted with a square-holed die. Choose three contrasting colours for each cane, rolling the selected colours into balls and pushing them together to form a plug. Extrude each plug in turn to create the canes, remembering to clean the extruder barrel after each use.

★★★ **Skill level**   🕐 **1–2 hours**   **Techniques:** *Wrapping and cutting seams p.14, Extruded cane p.19*

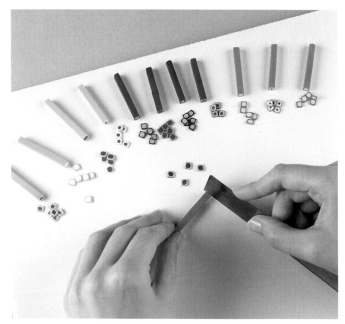

4 Using a sharp tissue blade, divide each cane into four sections and cut several slices from each, 1 mm ($^{1}/_{32}$ in) thick or less. The pattern changes along the length of a cane, so you will get more variety by taking slices from different parts of the cane – even though you may not need to use the entire cane.

5 Position the cane slices randomly over the clay rectangles, pushing each one down to adhere it to the base. Do not worry if some of the slices seem reluctant to stick to the surface – when the sheet is rolled smooth the leaf will crackle slightly, allowing the cane slice to bond with the clay beneath.

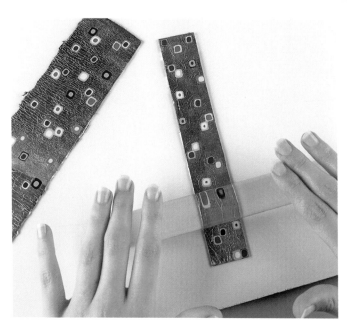

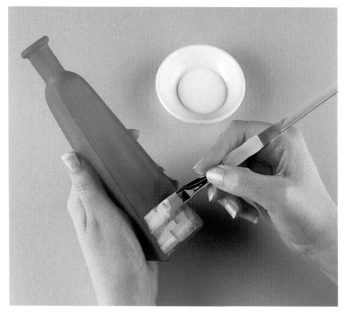

6 Roll the rectangles with a hand roller to sink the cane slices into the clay. Use a light touch, smoothing the slices in without rolling the clay base any thinner. Check both rectangles are still the correct width and make adjustments if necessary.

7 Brush a thin coating of PVA glue on to the bottom 8.5 cm ($3^{3}/_{8}$ in) of the glass bottle. The PVA glue keeps the unbaked clay in place as you work and will also help the clay to better adhere to the glass surface when it is baked. Allow the glue to partially dry until it is just tacky before proceeding to the next step.

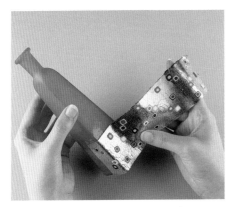

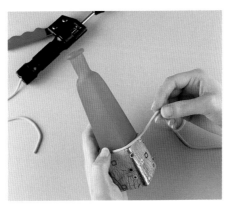

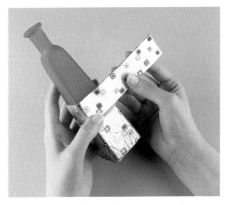

8 Wrap the gold rectangle around the base of the bottle, coaxing the clay to fit any tapers or curves in the glass and smoothing out air bubbles as you go. When the bottle is wrapped, trim away the overlapping clay and butt the cut edges together neatly. Ensure the top edge of the clay is perfectly horizontal, making adjustments with a craft knife if necessary.

9 Fit the extruder with the 3-mm (⅛-in)-diameter round-holed die and extrude the blue clay into a long string. Cut a length long enough to circle the bottle and apply to the glass just above the gold rectangle, hiding the cut edge of the clay. Try to keep all the seams together, starting and finishing the string where the rectangle starts and finishes.

10 Wrap the silver rectangle around the bottle, sitting it above the blue string. Work the clay into the contours of the glass as before, pushing out air bubbles as you go. Where the clay overlaps, trim a neat line and butt the cut edges together. When finished, check that the top of the clay is neat and level and then edge with more blue clay string to complete.

11 To make the stopper, roll a ball 25 mm (1 in) in diameter using the remaining blue clay. Cover in gold-coloured decorative leaf and roll between your hands to crackle the metal. Pinch the top into an onion shape and taper the base to fit the bottle. It does not need to be perfect; the stopper is purely decorative.

12 Stand the bottle on a baking tray and lay the stopper on a nest of batting beside it. Place into a cold oven and bring up slowly to the clay manufacturer's recommended baking temperature. When baked, allow the bottle to cool slowly. Varnish the metal-leafed areas to complete.

Templates All templates are actual size.

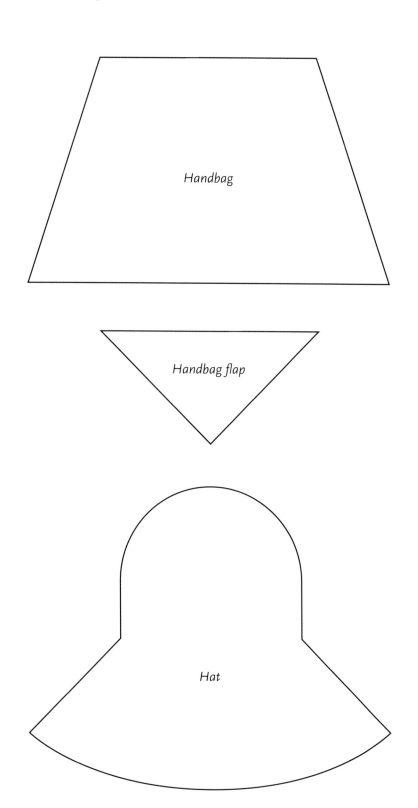

Handbag

Handbag flap

Hat

Hat and handbag greetings cards (pages 24-27)

Dragonfly gift tags (pages 40-43)

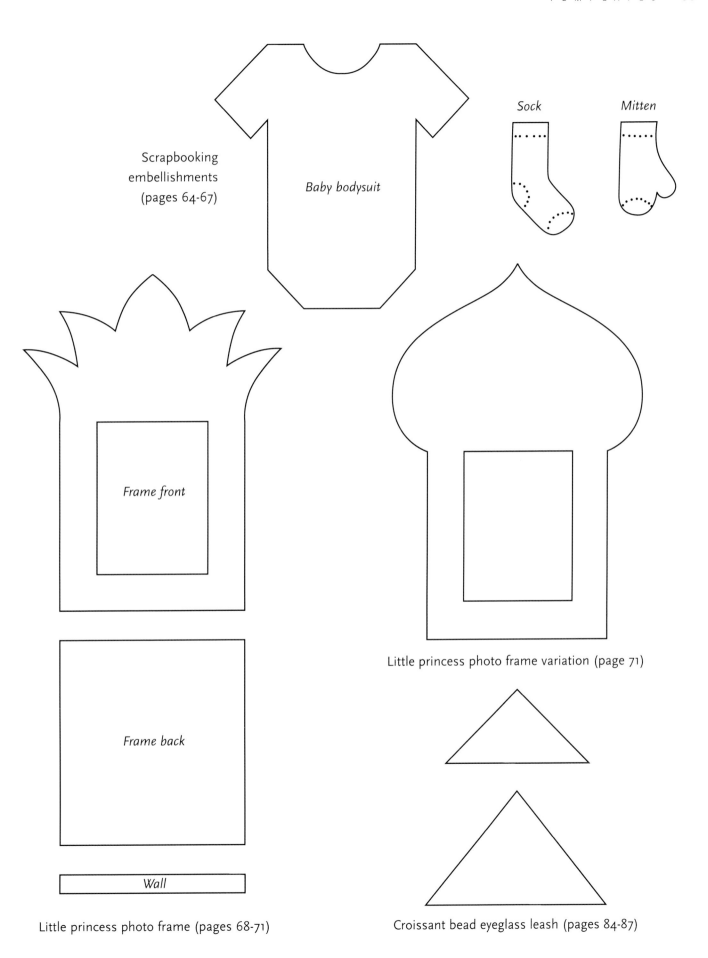

Scrapbooking embellishments (pages 64-67)

Baby bodysuit

Sock

Mitten

Frame front

Frame back

Wall

Little princess photo frame (pages 68-71)

Little princess photo frame variation (page 71)

Croissant bead eyeglass leash (pages 84-87)

Suppliers

UNITED KINGDOM

B & D Manufacturing Ltd/Tritools
15 Albert Road
Aldershot
Hampshire
GU11 1SZ
Tel: 01252 341 553
Email: Tritools1@aol.com
Manufacturer of sugarcraft extruders.

Craft Creations Ltd
Ingersoll House
Dalamare Road
Cheshunt
Hertfordshire
EN8 9HD
Tel: 01992 781 900
Email: enquiries@craftcreations.com
www.craftcreations.com
Supplier of greeting cards blanks and other card-making supplies.

E J R Beads
81 Woodcote Grove Road
Coulsdon
Surrey
CR5 2AL
Email: eralph@ejrbeads.co.uk
www.ejrbeads.co.uk
Supplier of beads, findings, Fimo polymer clay and craft supplies. Also home to Emma Ralph's own range of art focal beads.

Fred Aldous Ltd
37 Lever Street
Manchester
M1 1LW
Tel: 08707 517 300
Email: aldous@btinternet.com
www.fredaldous.co.uk
Craft supplies and tools.

George East Housewares Limited
Units 1-4A Masterlord Ind. Estate
Leiston
Suffolk
IP16 4JD
Tel: 01728 833 400
www.george-east.com

Hawthorne Hill
12 High Street
Knutton
Newcastle
Staffordshire
ST5 6DN
Tel: 01782 623 111
Email: info@hawthornehill.co.uk
www.hawthornehill.co.uk
Supplier of push moulds.

Homecrafts Direct
PO Box 38
Leicester
LE1 9BU
Tel: 0116 269 7733
www.homecrafts.co.uk
Supplier of cold enamel epoxy resins, wooden picture frames and other craft supplies and tools.

Oasis Art & Craft Products
Goldthorn Road, Kidderminster
Worcestershire
DY11 7JN
Tel: 01562 744 522
Distributor for Sculpey III and other Polyform products. Contact to find a retailer in your area.

Opitec Educational Materials Ltd.
Andersons Rd, Unit 51
Southampton
SO145FE
Tel: 02380 682 401
Email: info.uk@opitec.com
www.opitec.com
Selection of wind chimes and other craft supplies.

The Polymer Clay Pit
3 Harts Lane
Wortham,
Diss
Norfolk
IP22 1PQ
Tel: 01379 890 176
Email: info@polymerclaypit.co.uk
www.polymerclaypit.co.uk
Retailer of polymer clay, tools and supplies.

Specialist Crafts Ltd
PO Box 247
Leicester
LE1 9QS
Tel: 0116 269 7711
Email: post@speccrafts.co.uk
www.speccrafts.co.uk
Craft supplies and tools.

Staedtler (UK) Ltd
Pontyclun
Mid Glamorgan
CF72 8YJ
Tel: 01443 237 421
Email: marketing@uk.staedtler.com
www.staedtler.co.uk
Distributor for Fimo Classic, Fimo Soft, Fimo Liquid and Easy Metal decorative metal leaf. Contact to find your local retailer.

The Stamp Man
8a Craven Court
High Street
Skipton
North Yorkshire BD23 1DG
Tel: 01756 797 048
www.thestampman.co.uk
Unmounted rubber stamps, acrylic mounting blocks and other rubber stamping supplies.

EUROPE

Eberhard Faber GmbH
Postfach 1220
D-92302 Neumarkt
Germany
Tel: (09181) 430-0
www.eberhardfaber.de
Manufacturer of Fimo Classic, Fimo Soft, Fimo Gel and Easy Metal.

T&F Kunstoffe GmbH
Postfach 301236
D-63274 Dreieich
Germany
Manufacturer of Cernit.

USA

**Beryl's Cake Decorating
& Pastry Supplies**
P.O. Box 1584
N. Springfield
VA 22151-0584
Tel: (703) 256-6951
Email: beryls@beryls.com
www.beryls.com
*Retailer of sugarcraft extruders,
cookie cutters and Hawthorne Hill
push moulds.*

Craf-T Products
P.O. Box 83
Fairmont
MN 56031
www.craf-tproducts.com
*Supplier of decorating chalks. Contact
for nearest retailer.*

National Polymer Clay Guild (USA)
www.npcg.org
*Information on the national guild and
listings of regional guilds throughout
the United States.*

**Polymer Clay Express at
The ArtWay Studio**
13017 Wisteria Drive
Box 275
Germantown
MD 20874
Tel: (301) 482 0435
www.polymerclayexpress.com

Polyform Products Company
1901 Estes Avenue
Elk Grove Village
IL 60007
Tel: (847) 427-0020 ext. 29
www.polyformproducts.com
*Manufacturer of Premo! Sculpey,
Sculpey III, Translucent Liquid Sculpey
and other assorted polymer clay tools
and supplies.*

Rupert, Gibbon & Spider, Inc.
P.O. Box 425
Healdsburg
CA 95448
Toll Free: (800) 442-0455
Tel: (707) 433-9577
Email:
    service@jacquardproducts.com
www.jacquardproducts.com
*Manufacturer of Jaquard Pearl-Ex mica
pigment powders.*

Van Aken International
9157 Rochester Court
P.O. Box 1680
Rancho Cucamonga
CA 91729
www.katopolyclay.com
Manufacturer of Kato Polyclay.

AUSTRALIA

Cam Art, Science & Technology
197 Blackburn Rd
Mount Waverley
Victoria 3149
Tel: (03) 9802 4200
www.camartech.com.au

Modelene
www.modelene.com.au

Over the Rainbow
P.O. Box 495,
Ascot Vale,
Victoria 3032
Tel: (03) 9376 0545
Email: heather@polymerclay.com.au
www.polymerclay.com.au

NEW ZEALAND

Zigzag Polymer Clay Supplies Ltd
8 Cherry Place
Casebrook
Christchurch 8005
Tel: (03) 359 2989
Email: sales@zigzag.co.nz
www.zigzag.co.nz

Gordon Harris Art Supplies
4 Gillies Avenue
Newmarket
P.O. Box 26211
Auckland 1003
Tel: (09) 520 4466
Email:
    artsupplies@gordonharris.co.nz

Studio Art Supplies
81 Parnell Rise
Parnell
Auckland 1001
Tel: (09) 377 0302

The French Art Shop
33 Ponsonby Road
Ponsonby
Auckland 1003
Tel: (09) 376 0610

Littlejohns
170 Victoria Street
Wellington
Auckland 1003
Tel: (04) 385 2099
Email: Littlejohns@xtra.co.nz

Spotlight Stores
Locations throughout New Zealand:
Whangarei (09) 430 7220
Wairau Park (09) 444 0220
Henderson (09) 836 0888
Pamure (09) 527 0915
Manukau (09) 263 6760
Hamilton (07) 839 1793
Rotorua (07) 343 6901
New Plymouth (06) 757 3575
Hastings (06) 878 5223
Palmerston North (06) 357 6833
Porirua (04) 237 0650
Wellington (04) 472 5600
Christchurch (03) 377 6121
Dunedin (03) 477 1478
www.spotlight.net.nz
*Wide range of craft and decorative
painting supplies.*

Index